RIVERDISH

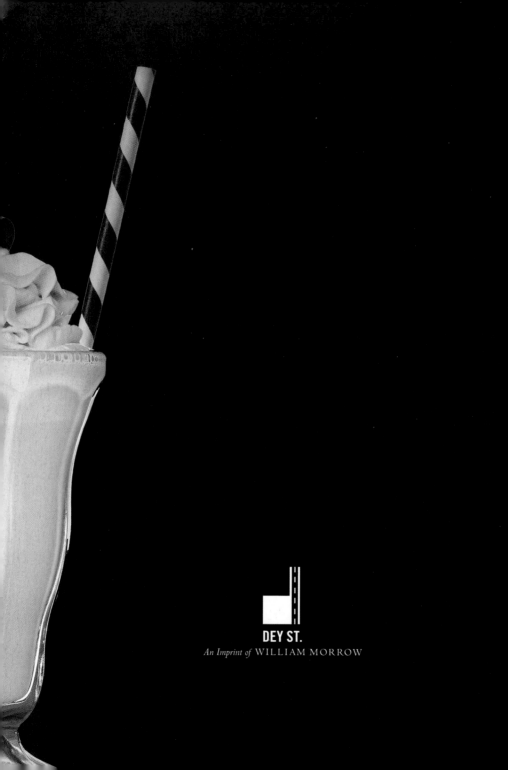

DEY ST.
An Imprint of WILLIAM MORROW

RIVERDISH

THE UNAUTHORIZED CASE FILES OF

RIVERDALE

RYAN BLOOMQUIST
& SAMANTHA GOLD

RIVERDISH. Copyright © 2019 by Ryan Bloomquist & Samantha Gold. All rights reserved. Printed in the United States of America. No part of this book may be used or reproduced in any manner whatsoever without written permission except in the case of brief quotations embodied in critical articles and reviews. For information, address HarperCollins Publishers, 195 Broadway, New York, NY 10007.

HarperCollins books may be purchased for educational, business, or sales promotional use. For information, please email the Special Markets Department at SPsales@harpercollins.com.

FIRST EDITION

Designed by Michelle Crowe

Library of Congress Cataloging-in-Publication Data has been applied for.

ISBN 978-0-06-290842-1

19 20 21 22 23   10 9 8 7 6 5 4 3 2 1

FOR NANA ROSE

CONTENTS

INTRODUCTION

Hey, River Vixens! It's Ryan and Sam, your hosts of *Riverdish*, coming at you in print! Since season one of *Riverdale*, we have gathered around a microphone with our friends and copious amounts of wine to discuss the goings-on in the crazy world of Riverdale. We have tried Jingle Jangle, threatened each other with sticky maples, and fangirled over the gay icon that is Nana Rose.

It all started one fateful Sunday afternoon when we sat down for a boozy brunch at Joanne Trattoria. *Yes, Lady Gaga's parents' restaurant. And no, she was not there. We were upset as well.*

Now, not to turn this book into a Yelp review, but you could say that our service that afternoon was worse than the "Jewels N' Drugs" track on *Artpop*. What should have been an hour-long meal eventually lasted three and inevitably led to us having one too many pitchers of mimosas.

Throughout our brunch, we could not stop chatting about the pilot we had watched for a new CW show called *Riverdale*. We'd both grown up obsessed with shows like *Pretty Little Liars* and *Gos-*

1

sip Girl, so the pilot had everything that we looked for in a television show—i.e., sexy teens and murder. With the help of some liquid courage and the microphone Ryan had recently purchased for his audition self-tapes, as well as the deep belief that there were others out there in the world who would have an interest in hearing what we had to say about this show, we went home that afternoon and pressed record, and *Riverdish* was born. Narcissism knows no bounds after multiple mimosa pitchers.

To be completely candid, when we recorded our first episode, Ryan had no idea that *Riverdale* was even based off a comic book series. Sam, being the good Jewish girl from Long Island that she is, had a vague recollection of the comic books from her summers spent at sleep-away camp. But neither of us would have considered ourselves massive *Archie* fans. How quickly that would change!

Before we knew it, this television show had consumed our lives. Our text conversations began to read like *Law & Order* scripts, as we desperately tried to parse out who murdered Jason Blossom. Every night, we would fall down rabbit holes, scouring the dark corners of the internet, reading every fan theory ever written about the show. We followed the cast on all their social media channels, hungry for any and all content concerning *Riverdale*. Thankfully for the sliver of our sanity that remains, it turned out that we were far from alone.

After its premiere, *Riverdale* very quickly became the leading network show among viewers ages eighteen to forty-nine. While the first season had a steady following, the network saw impressive spikes when the show's viewership grew more than 30 percent after launching on Netflix. When season two premiered, the demo rating and viewers more than doubled from the viewers who had watched the season one finale. More than 2.3 million viewers tuned in to the season two premiere alone!

Just as they had been for generations before us, the characters of Archie Andrews, Betty Cooper, Jughead Jones, and Veronica Lodge were once again at the forefront of popular culture. For Ryan, it is one of the few shows besides *CBS Sunday Morning* that he can actually talk about with his grandmother!

Yes, he is a devoted Sunday Morning fan.

Understandably, he does lose her slightly when he starts to discuss the serial killers and drug problems plaguing our favorite teens. Through *Riverdale*, our generation has been reintroduced to these iconic characters in a way in which they have never been portrayed before.

Now, as much as we adore this show, one thing that has always struck us about *Riverdale* is how incompetent the town law enforcement seems to be. No disrespect to Tom Keller, of course. We mean . . . have you *seen* his body? He could lock us up and we would *thank* him. But there is something so irresponsible about leaving the task of solving multiple homicides in the hands of teenagers who should be focused on school. Having traded so many theories back and forth about who is guilty of what, we have taken it upon ourselves to piece together the unofficial but essential crime files of *Riverdale*.

We suppose you could say that we were inspired by the detective skills of Jughead and Betty. Or maybe we were just jealous that they were living out the *Scooby-Doo* meets *True Detective* fantasy that we have always dreamed of. Perhaps this explains our obsession with escape rooms!

One time we were in an escape room that actually caught on fire! Being two theatrical people, we naturally assumed that the smoke pouring in from the outside door was all part of the room and were very impressed by the production values. By the grace of Nana Rose, we managed to escape just in time for the room supervisor to realize that we should escape the building. And that, our friends, is how you almost lost your Riverdish hosts.

If there is one thing that the history of *Riverdale* has shown us, it is that no one is innocent and that behind even the friendliest faces lie sinister aspirations.

Along with character profiles, we also have genuine photos from the scenes of some of Riverdale's most heinous crimes. Oh no, we are not just wannabe detectives trying to piece together these crimes while sitting at home! Our task of uncovering the truth behind the seedy underbelly of this town inspired us to pack up our suitcases and take a trip to the one and only Riverdale.

We can only hope that this information will inform and inspire fellow *Riverdale* detectives everywhere. Who knows? Maybe just like Betty Cooper, you too will receive an ominous call from a serial killer and the answers to his dark riddles will lie within these very pages. We mean, we certainly hope this *does not* happen to you, but one can never be too prepared!

One thing is for certain: no one in this town is completely innocent. Though the severity of their crimes may vary (not everyone is guilty of killing their own son), even the smallest offenses in this town deserve to be punished. ⟵

Shout-out to Betty Cooper's serpent dance.

Not to turn all Black Hood here, but he was not wrong when he called out all the residents in Riverdale as sinners. While we would never mess up our hair by donning a hood, we can continue to carry out his mission by keeping these hellions in check. Typically we like to operate under the assumption that people are innocent until proven guilty. In the case of Riverdale, however, experience has taught us time and time again that just the opposite seems to be true. And while it is not certain what lies in store for these characters, we do hope that these files will provide a blueprint for your own future sleuthing. Best of luck, and be careful around the Jingle Jangle.

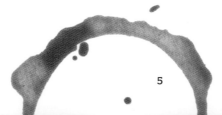

5

CASE FILE #1

ARCHIE ANDREWS

HEIGHT: 5'11"

AGE: 17

EYES: BROWN

PORTRAYED BY: KJ APA

Archie Andrews suffers from what we like to call pretty-boy syndrome. There is an old proverb that goes, "If you give a young teen abs, he will lose his brain." Okay, so maybe we made that up, but it still rings true. After working at his father's construction company over the summer before his sophomore year, Archie magically got ripped. Now, if those are the fitness results that you get from carrying wood and using a hammer, throw us a hard hat and put us to work! We have given half of our life savings to SoulCycle, and all we have to show for it is a graveyard of Smartwater bottles that we keep meaning to recycle.

Ultimately, Archie's main problem is that he is crippled by his own hero complex. Like so many other straight white men, he feels as though he is the solution to the world's problems. Let's call it like it is: he finds true satisfaction only when he is the hero of a situation. Take, for example, his stepping in at the Leopold and Loeb Juvenile Detention

The Leopold and Loeb Juvenile Detention Center is named after two infamous murderers, Nathan Leopold Jr. and Richard Loeb. Collectively known as Leopold and Loeb, the two young men were wealthy students at the University of Chicago who kidnapped and murdered a young boy in 1924 in an effort to commit what they perceived to be the "perfect crime." Appropriately enough, Leopold and Loeb were also featured players in showrunner Roberto Aguirre-Sacasa's play Golden Age, which was his first foray into the Archie universe. It somehow all makes perfect sense that the man who thought of putting a sexually confused Archie alongside Leopold and Loeb in a play would be the mind that would later go on to create Riverdale.

Center to save Joaquin from getting beaten to a pulp in the Pit. The warden realized that all you need to do to get Archie to do something is to let him feel as though he is saving the day.

Archie's situation is not helped by the fact that the female attention he receives is so unyielding. When the series first begins, he and Betty Cooper are sitting at Pop's Chock'lit Shoppe, with Betty trying to convey her feelings for him. Ever since playing together in the preschool sandbox, Archie Andrews and Betty Cooper have been the best of friends. Though the two of them would never admit it, most people in town would probably have put money down on the inevitability of Archie and Betty getting married. Two nice kids from well-respected families—it was the suburban dream! And it was hard to miss their obvious attraction to each other. Night after night they would stare out of their bedroom windows, looking for each other across the street. Occasionally, one would catch the other looking at the same time, only for both of them to quickly retreat to their beds—scared to let on that they were thinking of each other.

Before school started again, Betty wanted to tell Archie how she truly felt about him. If only our redheaded friend had not grown so distracted by the Big Apple bombshell who walked through the door. Enter Veronica Lodge. Veronica's eyes met Archie's instantly as if he were a Chanel sale at Bloomingdale's. Archie had never seen anyone so exotic looking in his life. In her black cape, Veronica looked straight out of Ivo van Hove's production of *The Crucible*. Archie was instantly smitten, and just like that, Varchie was born.

The Veronica, Betty, and Archie love triangle has divided Archie Comics fans for generations. Not since *Les Misérables* has a tale of unrequited love struck such a nerve in popular culture. (Cue an auto-tuned Betty singing "On My Own" in an inevitable *Les Miz* musical episode somewhere down the road.) While Ryan is very into the Veronica/Archie pairing that the show has been exploring, Sam still pines for the classic hometown-sweetheart relationship between Archie and Betty. Which is ironic, because both of us exclusively date Nick St. Clairs who make us feel bad about ourselves. It's nice to escape sometimes.

Okay, enough about love. We are here exploring crime, are we not? At first glance, Archie Andrews does not appear intelligent enough to screw in a lightbulb, let alone commit homicide. But could our redheaded friend have ulterior motives? We have watched *Showgirls* more than enough times to know that everyone has a Nomi Malone somewhere deep within. On closer inspection, the only person who stood in the way of Archie becoming the star of the Bulldogs was Jason Blossom. How convenient, then, that Jason would just mysteriously disappear one afternoon on Sweetwater River. Hell, Archie even ended up taking Jason's very own football number on the varsity team!

Archie's alibi in the murder case of Jason Blossom was essentially that he was more interested in his music career than he was in his football prospects. Oh, Archiekins, has the plight of Troy Bolton not taught you anything? This *never* ends well. We will give Archie credit where credit is due because it is rather impressive that he managed to teach himself guitar. The only instrument that either of us ever mastered was the recorder. But can we talk about those lyrics he wrote?! Archie's compositions read like a game of Mad Libs played between the nuns over at the Sisters of Quiet Mercy. We cannot topple the patriarchy until we stop giving untalented men opportunities simply because they show interest in fields that are not stereotypically masculine. Riverdale High has actual music superstars like Josie and the Pussycats! Why are we wasting time on this D-list Ed Sheeran?

We digress. It is easy to hate on Archie and all the questionable decisions that he makes, but when all is said and done, he does have a heart of gold. Remember when he punched through a sheet of ice with his own bare hands to rescue Cheryl Blossom?

Archie's chivalry really came through when the Black Hood came to town.

The music room! Riverdale High is blessed with many musically inclined students. Naturally, you must have a room in which to nurture those talents! By the way . . . have they found a replacement teacher for Ms. Grundy yet?

Fresh off an incredibly successful Riverdale jubilee the night before, Fred and Archie Andrews went for breakfast at Pop's. But before Pop Tate even had a chance to put the boys' eggs on the skillet, the morning was interrupted by a masked man with a gun.

At first, this seemed like one of those terrifying armed robberies that you hear about on the news. On closer inspection, however, it appeared as though something much larger was at play. For the gunman did not seem to be after anything in the cash register. Instead, he targeted Fred Andrews, shooting him and stealing his wallet.

The Andrews house! This is pretty much an exact replica of a real home in Vancouver that is used for all the exterior shots on the show.

The striking green eyes of this masked villain would forever be ingrained in Archie's memory. While most young teens would just be relieved that their father had survived, Archie could not forgive himself for letting his dad come that close to death. He made a pledge to himself that he would never allow harm to come Fred Andrews's way ever again.

Frustrated by what seemed to be a complete lack of interest from the town authorities in finding the gunman, Archie decided to take matters into his own hands. He became inspired after meeting Hiram Lodge at a *Matchlorette* viewing party hosted by Veronica. As someone with his fair share of run-ins with the law, Hiram informed Archie that when the police are not handling a situation, it is worthwhile to take matters into your own hands.

With his friends from the Bulldogs and a firearm from Dilton Doiley, Archie formed the Red Circle, a vigilante group focused on taking down the Black Hood. Instead of running away from fear, Archie chose to embrace it. Together, the group worked to keep the town safe from this masked man with sinister green eyes.

Of course, it was in trying to protect his father that Archie hurt Fred the most. We both have watched enough "meet the family" weeks on *The Bachelor* to know the importance of impressing your significant other's parents. That being said, we have never experienced this feeling ourselves, being that all our relationships have been shorter than Midge Klump's character arc, but we can imagine. Macho-man Archie insisted on impressing Hiram Lodge. And Hiram Lodge knew how to play Archie like a fiddle.

Before Archie knew it, he was playing Andy to Hiram's Miranda Priestly. Archie went from worrying about receiving a music scholarship to covering up the murders of mobsters like Poppa Poutine from Canada. And that's independent of the shady FBI agent who came to town to try to get dirt on Hiram Lodge through Archie. The Lodges' motives may be highly suspect, but we have to give it up to them. Hiring a man to pretend to be a government official just to see how much someone will talk about you behind your back is a boss move. For better or worse, Archie proved his loyalty to Hiram and passed his test with flying colors.

Yet, just when we thought that we could close our file on Archie Andrews, he became one of the only people in town to actually be charged with murder in the death of Cassidy Bullock.

Archie and the gang came into contact with Cassidy on their trip to the Lodge Lodge at Shadow Lake. Cassidy worked as a cashier at the local convenience store and was more than a little invested in the whereabouts of Betty and Veronica while they were in town. Later that evening he and his two buddies showed up to rob the Lodges' lake house, but not before Veronica could sneakily press the conveniently placed panic button under her dresser. If only Archie had not felt the need to once again prove his masculinity by chasing Cassidy into the woods after Cassidy ripped Veronica's necklace off her neck. Just seconds after Archie tackled Cassidy to the ground, he was interrupted by Andre, one of Hiram's assistants, who informed Archie that he would take care of the situation. As Archie walked back to the lodge, he heard the sound of a gunshot ringing through the woods.

A gunshot that Hiram Lodge would later use against Archie the first moment that Archie showed signs of wavering loyalty. In a major power move, Hiram decided to show Archie who was boss by having him arrested for the murder of Cassidy Bullock. We should note that the fact that Hiram now had complete control over the Riverdale police force and judicial system certainly helped his case against Archie.

Eventually, Archie pled guilty to the crime in order to not have to extend his trial after the jury failed to reach a conclusive decision. Listen, we have begrudgingly had to watch a few episodes of *The People's Court* in doctors' waiting rooms, but we have never seen someone want to get out of court so badly that they just pled guilty to a murder that they did not commit.

Of course, Archie did *not* kill Cassidy, but the fact that his DNA was all over Cassidy after their brawl didn't help his case. Hiram Lodge was well aware of this and framed Archie, even going so far as to kill the only other witness to Cassidy's murder, Andre, his own right-hand man.

A natural brunet, KJ Apa has stated that he can go about two weeks before he needs to dye his hair red again. Up until season three he also dyed his eyebrows. Scared that he would permanently lose them if production continued on this schedule, Apa now keeps his eyebrows his natural color. Appropriately enough, the actual *Archie* comic character has dark eyebrows! If anything, Apa's look has become closer to Bob Montana's original vision of Archie. Well, except for the abs. We like to imagine that Bob would not mind.

Archie had bought into Hiram's dog and pony show hook, line, and sinker and would now have to suffer the consequences. That is what happens when you get wrapped up with someone as cunning as Hiram Lodge. Archie might just be a dumb redbrick wall of abs, but he is *our* dumb wall of abs.

Never change, Archie Andrews.

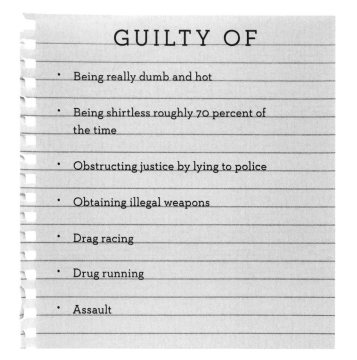

GUILTY OF

- Being really dumb and hot
- Being shirtless roughly 70 percent of the time
- Obstructing justice by lying to police
- Obtaining illegal weapons
- Drag racing
- Drug running
- Assault

VERONICA LODGE

HEIGHT: 5'2"

AGE: 17

EYES: BROWN

PORTRAYED BY: CAMILA MENDES

Not since Cady Heron's arrival to North Shore High School has a new student caused such a disruption in a school's social scene. Riverdale is located nowhere near a fault line, and yet Veronica Lodge's arrival registered high on the Richter scale. Not only did she interfere in Betty Cooper's conquest of Archie Andrews, she also changed the entire pecking order at Riverdale High. Cheryl Blossom, resident Head Bitch in Charge, may have run the River Vixens with an iron fist before Veronica, but even she was no match for the town's new Manhattan girl. Veronica even found her way into Josie and the Pussycats! Is there anything this girl cannot do? Her college application is going to look incredible. If she ever actually attends classes, that is.

Before moving to Riverdale, Veronica Lodge was the it-girl of New York City. She attended the Spence School on the Upper East Side of Manhattan and ruled the student body with a tenacity that would make Blair Waldorf shake. If there was a classmate's birthday party that she did not attend, it might as well have never happened. She was a ruthless bully, and rumor has it that the therapy bills of her peers were higher than the entire budget of Riverdale High. She sent one poor girl into such a tailspin that she had to transfer schools altogether.

Veronica's life seemed destined to be like so many others' in her friend group. Graduate high school, go on to attend an Ivy, use that degree to become a lifestyle blogger, and then eventually find a wealthy husband to have children with. She called it the Manhattan Circle of Life. There was one thing, however, that would forever set Veronica apart: her family name.

The Lodge family was legendary in New York City for all the wrong reasons. Hiram and Hermione Lodge ran Lodge Industries and lived their lives as if they were leads in *The Sopranos*. Let's just say that they had a standing reservation at Rao's. Justice, however, has a way of reaching even the most orderly of crime circles, and before Veronica's sophomore year, Hiram Lodge was incarcerated at the Yonkers Penitentiary for multiple counts of embezzlement and fraud.

Words cannot describe the embarrassment Veronica and Hermione felt the day that Hiram was carted off to prison. The rumors and gossip within the New York socialite circles quickly grew into a deafening roar, and rather than face their embarrassment head-on, Hermione decided to move back to her hometown of Riverdale.

They moved into the one piece of property in Hermione's name, a small pied-à-terre in the Pembrooke. If you were a child who grew up in Riverdale, the Pembrooke was a building that you were bound to know. Set among the mom-and-pop stores of Main Street, the Pembrooke stuck out like a sore thumb. With its Roman columns and marble facade, the building itself seemed to spit in the face of everything that Riverdale stood for. Rumors abounded as to what the building was even doing there in the first place. It was only on very rare occasions that you would see anyone going in or out. Once in a blue moon, you might catch the doorman, Smithers, stepping out for a breath of fresh air, but otherwise the Pembrooke's purpose in town was widely unknown. It therefore served as quite a shock when the Lodges' black Escalade pulled up in front of the building one early September night.

At first glance, it would seem as though we could clear Veronica's name of all crimes in town. (Well, everything except for wearing her pearls into the shower.) She did not even know Jason Blossom! What motive would she have had to aid in his murder? And as for the Black Hood murders, there was no way that Veronica was going

The Pembrooke is actually the Permanent building—a registered heritage building located in downtown Vancouver that has been transformed into an event space, available for private bookings! The showy exterior is perfect for the Lodges' ritzy digs.

to ruin her blowout by donning a hood. Does Riverdale even have a Drybar? Still, we can't ignore the fact that it was only after Veronica arrived in town that everything started to go awry. Although Veronica herself may not have personally killed anyone, her family has a criminal history the length of a CVS receipt.

Their criminal past grew all too apparent when Hiram Lodge returned to town and started to develop his SoDale project. Even Veronica grew wary of her parents' master plan. The situation is not ideal if you reach the point of accusing your parents of hiring a hit man to take out your boyfriend's father. It seemed as though the closer Veronica became with her parents, the more glaring their wrongdoings became in her eyes. SoDale was no innocent housing project. Rather, it was simply a cover-up for Hiram Lodge's complete monopolization of the Southside. Hiram had planned to turn Southside High into a for-profit prison complex and the housing at SoDale was to be used as housing for the prison's employees. As if Riverdale did not have enough crime, Hiram aimed to deliberately bring criminals to town for the sole purpose of personal financial gain for himself. There are not enough Cristal mimosas in the world to help deal with that sort of stress.

The young teens of Riverdale suffer from a staggering amount of daddy issues, but maybe no one more so than Veronica Lodge. It is understandable. We mean, imagine your father roping your high school boyfriend into his criminal empire, forcing him to start a homegrown vigilante group, and then sending him to jail for a murder that he did not commit? We thought we had it bad when we had to pretend to enjoy the sports games that our dads took us to!

Veronica Lodge's room!

Say what you will about Veronica, but you cannot deny her determination to take control of her own life. At the young age of seventeen she declared herself financially independent from her parents and became a small-business owner with La Bonne Nuit, her speakeasy under Pop's. At this point, Veronica is just trying to keep her head above water among the turmoil that has come her way. In the span of two years she has uprooted her entire life, seen her boyfriend be sent off to prison, and witnessed her two parents ruthlessly take over an entire small town. We feel confident in clearing Veronica's name for the time being. But how long will it take before she realizes that it is much easier to get ahead in life by *not* following the rules? Will Veronica ultimately follow her parents' footsteps into organized crime? Only time will tell.

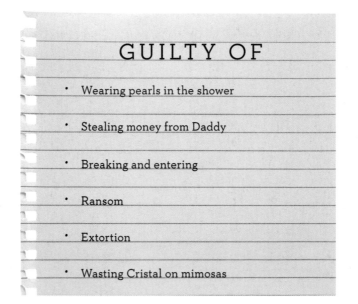

GUILTY OF

- Wearing pearls in the shower

- Stealing money from Daddy

- Breaking and entering

- Ransom

- Extortion

- Wasting Cristal on mimosas

CASE FILE #3

BETTY COOPER

HEIGHT: 5'6"

AGE: 17

EYES: GREEN

PORTRAYED BY: LILI REINHART

lizabeth "Betty" Cooper might seem like your classic, all-American girl next door, but underneath her tight blond ponytail, there is much more than meets the eye. While we are all about a *You Belong with Me*–era Taylor Swift–type chick, everyone knows the most innocent-seeming people keep the most sinister secrets. Inevitably, a *Reputation* era is just around the corner, serpents and all.

Betty was born and raised in Riverdale and grew up alongside her older sister, Polly. Together, they lived out a white-picket-fence fantasy under the watchful eyes of their parents, Hal and Alice Cooper. While the girls grew up, Alice was extremely controlling and pushed Betty and Polly toward her idea of perfection. Have we learned nothing from Stephen Sondheim's *Into the Woods*? If you are overbearingly protective of your children, eventually they are going to leave their tower and you will be left alone to belt out an incredible ballad before disappearing into a cloud of smoke.

Although not necessarily an ivory tower in which Betty was locked up, Betty's bedroom felt pretty similar as she sat there night after night, pining for Archie Andrews across the street. Alice had a habit of monitoring everything, including, but not limited to, Betty's clothes, grades, appearance, and friends. She even got Betty an Adderall prescription so that she could focus on schoolwork.

Alice Cooper does eventually end up singing a similar ballad about learning to let a child go during the musical episode! Actress Mädchen Amick has stated that she was initially terrified to sing in the episode, but we must say that she ended up doing a lovely job. Of course, we are still upset that we never got Margaret White singing "And Eve Was Weak." We will have to take that one up with Kevin Keller.

It takes a certain type of monster to make Mama Rose look sweet. Betty's home life was an emotional pressure cooker that was close to exploding.

It was the extraordinary pressure that Betty was faced with that led her to discovering her alter ego, Dark Betty. Yes, the Dark Betty story line does feel slightly heavy-handed, but let's keep in mind that she is being raised by an overly controlling mother and serial killer

Yes. That is the iconic window in which it was proclaimed that Archie did, in fact, get hot!

father, so we can cut Betty some slack. We first met Dark Betty when Chuck Clayton asked Veronica out on a date and then proceeded to have the audacity to Photoshop a picture of them together with maple syrup all over Veronica's face. Veronica learned that this is what the residents of Riverdale refer to as a "sticky maple," an outrageous form of slut shaming that insinuates the sexual things that allegedly occurred on their date. In reality, all that Veronica and Chuck did was kiss, and the image of them being spread all around Riverdale High was, and still is, fake news.

Enraged by Chuck's treatment of her friend, Betty donned an old wig that she found in Veronica's wardrobe and decided to teach Chuck a lesson.

We like to think that this wig is probably from a production of Cabaret that Veronica did at Spence, in which she played Sally Bowles.

As soon as Betty put on the wig, she felt different. With some leftover Christmas money, she purchased

PBteen, eat your heart out! Betty
Cooper's bedroom is #goals.

black lingerie, and just like that the Dark Betty look was complete.
She handcuffed Chuck Clayton to a hot tub and gave him a literal
sticky maple of his own, almost drowning him in the process.

Once you feel this sort of power, it is hard to rein it back in. Hal
Cooper knew this feeling well and took full advantage by enticing
Betty with it once he began communicating with her as the Black
Hood.

We would love to see some transcripts of Betty's cam-girl conversations. Who was she even talking to, and what exactly was she saying? Is it weird that we can't stop thinking about this? Yes, it's weird.

Betty's dark side wasn't just
talk. Let's not forget that she
helped her mother cover up a
murder, turned her fake brother
over to a serial killer, and casually became a cam girl.

Betty even revealed this darker side of herself to her boyfriend, Jughead, in the bedroom. We are certainly not here to kink shame. Whatever floats your boat, we are in full support of. But the last time one of us wore a wig in the bedroom was during Sam's star-making performance in her high school production of *The Wedding Singer*, in which she played Linda and seduced the lead.

Speaking of Jughead and Betty, we suppose that we should acknowledge the surprise power

Can we just talk for a second about how crazy it is that Betty doesn't have her phone on silent? What kind of psychopath has their phone on anything other than vibrate? We understand having a loud ringtone if you are older or some sort of emergency doctor. But other than that, there is no reason that your phone should ring. Hell, we could not tell you what our ringtones even are! Though after watching Riverdale we are tempted to make it "Lollipop" just for shits and giggles.

Still to this day Ryan is frustrated by the pressure of societal gender norms that forced him to read the Hardy Boys over Nancy Drew! It was like when waiters used to force him to get a Roy Rogers drink instead of a Shirley Temple. Maybe he just prefers the taste of sprite and grenadine over Coke?!

couple of Riverdale High. Once Veronica swooped in and snatched up Archie, Betty set her sights on Jughead Jones. Well, not so much set her sights on as happened into during their investigation into the murder of Jason Blossom. Just like her mother, Betty has always had a penchant for journalism. As soon as she roped Jughead into helping her restore Riverdale High's newspaper, *The Blue and Gold*, the two became inseparable. It was as if Nancy Drew started dating Joe Hardy.

With local law enforcement proving to be both corrupt and rather incompetent, Jughead and Betty set out to solve every crime in town.

While this would seem to clear their names of crime, there is so much more to Betty Cooper than her preppy basics and big green eyes. As the great Britney Spears once said, she's not that innocent. If the Black Hood proved anything, it was that the darkness within her went much deeper than even she knew. She might be safe from prosecution when it comes to the crimes of Riverdale for now, but seeing as it was her speech at the town jubilee that inspired the Black Hood's killing spree, we have a feeling that Dark Betty is definitely one to keep a watchful eye on.

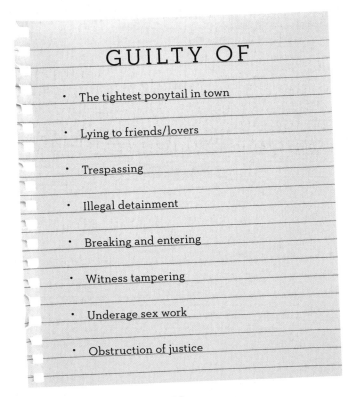

GUILTY OF

- The tightest ponytail in town
- Lying to friends/lovers
- Trespassing
- Illegal detainment
- Breaking and entering
- Witness tampering
- Underage sex work
- Obstruction of justice

CASE FILE #4

JUGHEAD JONES

HEIGHT: 6'0"

AGE: 17

EYES: BLUE

PORTRAYED BY: COLE SPROUSE

F orsythe Pendleton Jones III, Riverdale's resident recluse. Or, as he's better known, Jughead Jones. Jughead is like if you combined the broody hipster guy you went to school with who only listened to indie bands with Sherlock Holmes. Not necessarily the ingredients for the most popular kid in high school, but Jug makes it work. Most of his spare time is spent holed up in Pop's working on what is sure to be the next great American novel. You see, Jughead is different from the other characters in this tale. While his classmates grew up convinced of the idyllic nature of their small town, he always knew better.

Behind every smile is a beast. Human nature is such that we are built to be both Jekyll and Hyde. While we are Jekylls most of the time, there is always a Hyde in us waiting to jump out at any moment. ⟵ *Or at least this is what Ryan took away from the regional production of Jekyll and Hyde that he did a few years ago.*

Jughead learned this lesson at an early age. Although he grew up alongside Archie and Betty, his parents were far from the community leaders that the Andrewses and Coopers proved to be. His father, FP Jones, was the leader of the Southside Serpents, the local gang in town that constantly bucked up against the so-called upstanding residents of Riverdale. He also suffered terribly from alcoholism. When Jughead was young, his mother finally had enough and moved to Toledo with his sister, Jellybean, in tow. Yet there was something that made Jug stay behind in Riverdale. Perhaps it was the fact that he did not want to live beyond a five-mile radius of a Pop's burger, or perhaps it was fate. He found refuge at the Twilight Drive-In and raised himself.

From a fan perspective, it is hard not to fall in love with Jughead. While it certainly does not hurt that Cole Sprouse is such a looker, the show also invites us to see beyond the lone-wolf stereotype that others in town might cast upon him. In terms of following leads regarding the crimes in Riverdale, however, we must admit that Jughead does seem to check a whole lot of boxes when it comes to potential killers. If we put ourselves in Sarah Koenig's shoes and went to Riverdale to record a season of *Serial*, we would want Jughead Jones as one of our first interviewees.

Side note: How incredible would a Sarah Koenig-esque character be on *Riverdale*? Jughead and Betty would feel totally threatened by this new addition of competition for what seems to be their monopoly on crime-solving, and for us, it would be an opportunity to hire an older character actress, which always makes our hearts very happy.

Jughead has all the makings of a small-town killer: parental issues, loner, white male, and a history of being bullied by the murder victim. Though if Jughead were responsible for the killings, why would he devote all his energy to solving his own crimes? While we do not put it beyond the show to give us a plot twist like this, in Jughead's case it seems highly unlikely.

Of course, Jughead was not alone in his crime-solving sleuthing. It was through trying to find out who murdered Jason Blossom that Jug fell in love with Betty Cooper. The boys of *True Detective* have nothing on these two!

Showrunner Roberto Aguirre-Sacasa has stated that season three of *Riverdale* is heavily influenced by *True Detective*.

Jughead and Betty first truly connected when Betty approached Jug to write for the school newspaper, *The Blue and Gold.*

Together, they were able to uncover the truth behind the gunfire at Sweetwater River, rid the town of a child predator, and discover the real reason why Jason would have faked a disappearance on the morning of July 4th. And of course, who could forget how they exposed the dark, sticky truth of how Clifford Blossom murdered Jason, his own son?

The *Blue and Gold* office! Not too shabby for a school paper.

Just when Jughead thought that he was going to be able to hang up his signature crown beanie, his investigations into the seedy underbelly of Riverdale turned even more intense with the arrival of the Black Hood and Gargoyle King. This poor kid just couldn't catch a break. It was one thing for a father to kill his own son over family drama. But when the Black Hood arrived in town and started mercilessly killing innocent citizens left and right, it became clear that much darker forces were at play.

As if the increasing intensity of his crime investigations were not enough, Jughead was also forced to transfer to Southside High. While this dismayed him at first, it wasn't long until he started to feel right at home. He was able to continue his journalism career by relaunching the school's newspaper, *The Red and Black*, and discovered a new muse in Toni Topaz.

Not only did he find comfort in school, he also grew increasingly involved in his extracurricular activities with the Southside Serpents. Growing up, Jughead had his fair share of issues with the Serpents. He was witness to the tight grasp they had on his father, and without a doubt, many of their practices were beyond suspect. But by spending more time on the Southside, Jughead began to see that quite often, the Serpents simply got a bum rap. With his father, FP, still in jail, Jughead very quickly climbed the ranks of the Serpents

The iconic beanie Jughead wears throughout the series is an homage to the crown the character sports in the comics! Believe it or not, through at least season two, Cole Sprouse had only one beanie that he used throughout the entirety of shooting. As you can imagine, it acquired quite a repugnant smell over time. Production eventually did create a duplicate beanie, but it was quickly stolen from the set. In some ways, we are sure that Jug's smelly beanie helps Cole get into character some. Not to generalize, but Jughead doesn't seem like the type of guy who is diligent about doing his laundry.

and became the group's leader. As Shakespeare said in *Henry IV, Part 2*, "Uneasy lies the head that wears a crown."

It is often said that you become the company you keep, and Jughead was no exception. Without his meaning it to, the Serpents' lifestyle of crime that he so despised soon became his own. Lesson learned: never get in bed with a snake charmer, as the snake will always bite back. Enter Penny Peabody.

Penny is a cagey attorney the Serpents keep on call in case of any legal issues. She lives by Hammurabi's ancient "an eye for an eye, a tooth for a tooth" code, and instead of cash, Penny prefers payments in the form of favors. Naturally, most of these favors tend to coincide with her drug-trafficking operation, in which she transports drugs (aka "pancake mix") from the Southside to Greendale. According to Penny, things had taken a turn for the worse with FP in prison. Jughead's one chance to have his father's sentence reduced would be to follow Penny's orders by taking one shipment of pancake mix for her to Greendale.

With the assistance of Farmer McGinty and Archie, Jug completed Penny Peabody's task, but his celebration was short-lived. For when he and Archie reached the Greendale warehouse, Jug realized just how deeply embedded in Penny's operation he had become. It turns out that there was no attack on his father in prison. Penny lied to Jughead to get him to do what she wanted and now possessed video footage of him delivering drugs. Yes, Penny holding this blackmail over Jughead was certainly less than ideal, but Jughead's choice to then skin Penny of her Ser-

It's like we always say, you can ghost a bad hookup all you want, but eventually you will run into each other at Starbucks.

pent tattoo and leave her in a ditch in Greendale was probably not the best plan of action. Jughead is intelligent enough to know that eventually this will backfire on him.

For as skilled as Jughead is as an amateur detective, we cannot let him off that easily for the actual crimes he has committed. He might play all coy and non-attention seeking, but the deeper you dig into Jug, the more apparent his hunger for power becomes. First he finagles his way into becoming the Serpent King after mere weeks in the Serpents, and then he insists on being the game leader of Gryphons and Gargoyles. This is someone who likes to be in control of the narrative. We mean . . . he is our narrator, after all.

In some ways we feel bad that Jug has to be constantly on the go, hunting down criminals. Life seemed a whole lot simpler back when his only duty was to work the screen projector at the Twilight and scarf down burgers at Pop's. On the other hand, however, how incredible is it that he has all this material to work with for his novel? Authors only dream about finding plotlines this rich. Keep writing, Jug! We cannot wait to read it.

GUILTY OF

- Leading a gang
- Being a terrible writer
- Drug running
- Drag racing
- Vandalism
- Trespassing
- Breaking and entering
- Constantly brooding

CASE FILE #5

CHERYL BLOSSOM

HEIGHT: 5'6"

AGE: 17

EYES: BROWN

PORTRAYED BY: MADELAINE PETSCH

Regina George. Heather Chandler. Sharpay Evans. Every high school needs a self-proclaimed queen bee, and for Riverdale High, Cheryl Blossom easily snatches the crown.

It's only fitting that the queen bee is a Blossom—the Blossom family is one of the founding families of Riverdale. Nearly one hundred years ago the Blossoms established the Blossom Maple Farms to almost immediate success, and under the family's leadership, the maple syrup industry became the driving force of Riverdale's economy. In this town, like so many others, money talks, and whatever the Blossoms say, goes. It's widely known that power corrupts, and that absolute power corrupts absolutely. As for Cheryl, her unchecked power within the town made her a force to be reckoned with.

Gorgeous, entitled, and rich, Cheryl has a confidence that could kill. She is head cheerleader of the River Vixens and basically every word uttered from her mouth is instantly iconic. She might be known as a mean girl, but what can we say? We stan Cheryl Blossom.

Of course, like many people who appear to have it all, Cheryl has struggled with her fair share of hidden demons. It is not easy losing a brother, especially one you were so close with.

But the loss cuts extra deep when you were the one partially responsible for it. Cheryl was only trying to do the right thing for her brother when she helped him stage his disappearance from Riverdale. But she unknowingly led him straight into the arms of his captor and his untimely death. There are some things in life that we just can-

Like . . . SUPER close. We cannot be the only ones who were slightly creeped out by the almost romantic bond that the series explored early on between Jason and Cheryl, right?!

not control. Jason's dead body washing up on the shore of the river was an unexpected and tragic surprise that will haunt Cheryl for the rest of her life.

Cheryl's moody, dark cherry bedroom is EVERYTHING!

While a normal and loving parent would typically be able to talk a child down from this overbearing sense of guilt, Penelope is no normal parent. Jason Blossom was the golden boy of the family, and Cheryl served as the perfect scapegoat for Penelope to take all her aggression out on. Little did Penelope know that the real monster she should have been upset with was her own husband. Just put yourself in Cheryl's shoes and imagine how you would feel if, after being blamed for your brother's death for months, you finally discovered that it was your own father who killed him. We mean . . .

Sam alone has three therapists. Can we not find Cheryl one? This poor girl is going to need as much help as she can get.

In an effort to deal with this trauma, she attempted to drown herself in Sweetwater River. Thankfully she was rescued by Archie and the gang. But she then proceeded to burn down her family mansion in an effort to create a blank slate. Cheryl has never been one to shy away from the dramatics, but this seems a bit much even for her.

Can we move into Cheryl Blossom's closet? Please and thank you!

Fact: Cheryl is hot. With her long, flowing ginger locks and banging bod, she can get any guy she wants at Riverdale High. She flirts to manipulate and feigns interest in those she deems suitable (we're looking at you, Nick St. Clair!). But turns out, it's not the guys she's interested in. Back when Cheryl was in junior high, she befriended a girl in her class named Heather whom she began hanging out and having sleepovers with. This closeness soon shifted into something deeper. One night, Penelope Blossom caught Cheryl and Heather in bed together. Furious that her "perfect" daughter had disgraced the family name, she banished Heather from Cheryl's life.

Like most other mean girls, Cheryl's bitchiness was really just armor to protect her vulnerable heart. The armor that she built, however, made it difficult for her to keep friends. This was never made more apparent than in her friendship with Josie McCoy. The two first got close after Cheryl recruited Josie to the Vixens. With all the trauma in Cheryl's life, it's natural she gets a bit possessive of people, but she took this desire a step too far after Chuck Clayton expressed interest in Josie. Cheryl went into full-on stalker mode, threatening Josie with drawings and "gifts" (including a pig heart)

in her locker. Eventually, Josie learned her stalker was Cheryl and rightfully kept her distance until the two reconnected when forced to duet in *Carrie: The Musical.* Ah, musical theater. How it solves any and every problem. We truly believe if everyone were able to break out in song when faced with confrontation, we would have world peace.

While Cheryl still struggles some with maintaining friendships, she thankfully has come into her own with regard to romantic relationships. This change was brought on by Toni Topaz. Toni has a way of removing

Love a spooky boudoir moment.

Cheryl's armor and seeing her for who she truly is. From the moment the two of them met, sparks flew. (We're not crying; *you're* crying.) History, however, has a habit of repeating itself, and the instant that Penelope caught Toni and Cheryl together she went into full-on Miss Trunchbull mode. She pulled Cheryl from the school musical and sent her to conversion therapy at the Sisters of Quiet Mercy. I mean, hasn't the girl been through ENOUGH?! Thankfully, as Taylor Swift's "Bad Blood" video proves, there is nothing stronger than a girl gang. Veronica, Toni, and Kevin break Cheryl out of the home, and in that moment, Cheryl decides she is out for revenge. The first thing she does? Become a Serpent. (In a one-of-a-kind Red Serpent jacket, no less.)

Cheryl may have her demons, but she seems much more an asset to the crime-fighting mystery gang than a suspect herself. She might sin while seeking to bring her family to justice but honestly, who can really blame her?

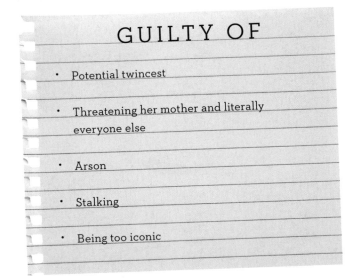

GUILTY OF

- Potential twincest
- Threatening her mother and literally everyone else
- Arson
- Stalking
- Being too iconic

KEVIN KELLER

HEIGHT: 5'11"

AGE: 17

EYES: GREEN

PORTRAYED BY: CASEY COTT

I n the pilot episode of *Riverdale*, Veronica meets Kevin Keller for the first time in the school hallway and says something to the effect of "Thank god, you're gay. Let's be best friends." We could not agree more, Veronica. Kevin Keller's appearances on this show are like when "One Day More" gets played at Marie's Crisis. Even though you know it is bound to happen, it never fails to delight. Out of all the characters on the show he serves as the audience surrogate in this crazy world. We are slightly upset that we have yet to venture inside the town's one gay bar, Innuendo, but for the time being we suppose that we will have to deal with La Bonne Nuit being the town's most queer-centric space. (Well, that and every single wrestling match.)

This poor kid! Every time he tries to get off, he is interrupted by murder. We have had some bad hookups, but nothing to the extent that Kevin has gone through. It is truly enough to make you never want to have sex again. Well, unless you are into your sexual adventures ending in murder, in which case, we would like to encourage you to put down this book and talk to a professional.

For the most part, Kevin appears to be the town's resident good boy. But a closer look at Kevin reveals that he has much more going on than meets the eye. First of all, it is hard to ignore the fact that he always seems to be at the scene of the crime when bodies are found. It was on the night of the school semiformal when he and Moose went for—ahem—a "night swim" and discovered Jason Blossom's body washed up on the shore of Sweetwater River. Just mere months later, Kevin was out in Fox Forest—ahem—"night jogging" when he heard the Black Hood shooting Moose and Midge in the distance.

44

We suppose now is also the time when we should address Kevin's habit of cruising in the woods. Although we are incredibly sympathetic to Kevin's plight of being the only out gay male at Riverdale High, he has to know that there are better ways to get some action than by hooking up with random strangers in the forest. That being said, it is impressive that Riverdale has this sort of culture to begin with. There was no cruising culture in our hometowns! Well, at least none that we knew of.

One of our favorite parts of the entire series is Kevin's monologue to Betty after she spoke with Kevin's dad about his cruising behind his back. Kevin explained that while Betty had the option of going to Jughead's trailer and getting her fix on his ratty couch any time she pleased, he had far fewer options.

The couch where it happened! Yes, there are probably more romantic places to lose your V-card, but who are we to judge?!

All that is to say, it is not as though Kevin has not had his fair share of action. We have ranked his boyfriends to date here from worst to best.

FANGS FOGARTY

We have to rank the relationship between Fangs and Kevin last since it never really left the ground. While it was hinted at quite often in season two, we did not get much more than the occasional wink between them. Though when Fangs first introduced himself to Kevin, he made sure to stress that he was old friends with Joaquin. Is there a world where Fangs and Joaquin had a fling and now they have both ended up coming to Kevin for sloppy seconds? Fangs even had the nerve to serve as Kevin's assistant director for *Carrie: The Musical* while he was hooking up with Midge Klump. Kevin deserves better, though Fangs is a total hottie.

JOAQUIN

We like Joaquin for Kevin in a very Danny-and-Sandy-in-*Grease* sort of way. And not just because we think Kevin would look super cute in a leather jacket! These two lovebirds first locked eyes at the Twilight Drive-In snack stand. And as they often do, this brief encounter quickly escalated into an intense back-alley make-out session. Of course, there was the tiny snag that Kevin was the sheriff's son and Joaquin was a member of the Southside Serpents. Ultimately the truth comes out that at first Joaquin was dating Kevin only so that he could get inside information for the Serpents on the Jason Blossom murder investigation. While he later confesses to Kevin that he ended up feeling a true connection with him, this raises enough red flags in our mind to make us worried. It would be like us dating a guy just for access to his Hamptons house over the summer and then trying to manufacture a connection after Labor Day. Nothing against people with a criminal record, but we think that we prefer someone a little more wholesome for our boy Kevin.

MOOSE MASON

We ship Koose/Mevin (we are still workshopping their couple name) all the way. We do not know if it is simply because Moose was Kevin's OG buddy, but he is by far our favorite option. Yes, Moose is struggling with finding his sexuality, but that is just a natural part of getting through puberty. All he needs is for someone to give him permission to step into his authentic self and we could see him having all the makings of a wonderful boyfriend. We are hoping that Kevin could be the person to give him that permission. While we would have preferred Midge to not have been murdered onstage, at least she is now out of the picture and all our couple goals for Kevin and Moose can come true.

Just like us fans at home, cast members on Riverdale have no idea what the fates of their characters are until they receive a script for each episode. Cody Kearsley, who plays Moose, assumed that his character was dead after reading the scene in which he and Midge are shot in their car. It was not until he received a script for the following episode that he learned he survived! Talk about job stress!

Speaking of Midge Klump's death during Kevin's production of *Carrie*, we should mention an ancient tradition that is beloved by the theater community. We are, of course, referring to blaming the director when things go wrong. In the theater, when actors are lauded for a great performance, they happily take all the credit. Talk to an actor about a bad performance, however, and it is almost always the fault of their director.

Sure, Kevin might not have purposefully orchestrated the Black Hood's attack that night, but he certainly would have had reason enough to do so. First Midge Klump stole Moose from him, and then she had the audacity to start hooking up with Kevin's one other love prospect, Fangs?! It would seem as though Midge had a type.

Considering that Sam's boyfriends all the way through college ended up being gay, she is in no place to judge.

Perhaps Kevin's first mistake was his choice of musical itself. Don't get us wrong, we love *Carrie*! Unfortunately, the show has just never carried the best of luck with it. In the late '80s, *Carrie* was presented on Broadway and lasted only twenty-one performances. Ever since, it has lived on in show-queen lore. Of course, Kevin Keller (who we are sure is a frequent visitor on the Broadway World message boards) would have grown up obsessed with the bootleg audio of Betty Buckley singing "And Eve Was Weak." And in a town plagued by a serial killer, it does track that Riverdale High would present something a bit edgier than *Bye Bye Birdie*.

If only Kevin had known that this production would prove to be even more disastrous than the show's original Broadway run. It turns out Riverdale High had its very own Phantom of the Opera, but this one covered more than part of his face.

BRB . . . just dream-casting a Riverdale High School Players production of Bye Bye Birdie. Dilton Doiley was practically born to play Hugo Peabody. And if KJ Apa's moves in Carrie are any indication, we think he has just the right amount of swagger in his hips to serve as an incredible Conrad Birdie. (KJ Apa is known to step into many different alter egos while hanging out on set. During the filming of the musical episode, he fully embraced his musical theater, jazz-hand-loving side with an alter ego that the cast lovingly named Fifi. We can only hope that Fifi will get the chance to come out again!)

The soundstage that *Riverdale* films on is separated into three different stages. Along with the sets, there is also an office section at the front of the building where all the departments have working spaces. Throughout the office hallways, you'll find old posters that were once used on the show. Here, of course, you see an audition notice for *Carrie: The Musical*. We always hated staying after school on Fridays, but getting to audition for this production would have been worth it!

The writing was on the wall from day one of rehearsal, when a sandbag mysteriously dropped from the ceiling and nearly killed Cheryl Blossom. Later, when Kevin found a letter from the Black Hood claiming that it was he who dropped the bag and demanding that the role of Carrie White be recast, he naturally assumed that it was somebody playing a joke. The casting of school musicals can always turn contentious, and throughout history people in show business have gone to great lengths to fight for roles.

At the time, the letter seemed more like the work of a bitter ensemble member than the Black Hood himself, though as the production went on, it became evident that we were dealing with something much more serious than just your regular Eve Harrington.

Looking at you, Ivy Lynn and Karen Cartwright!

Against his will, Kevin eventually did recast the role of Carrie with Cheryl's understudy, Midge Klump. Seemingly the only force more menacing than the Black Hood is Penelope Blossom, and without her giving permission to let Cheryl continue in the show, Principal Weatherbee would not have allowed the production to continue.

Excitement over stepping into the lead role soon turned to terror for poor Midge Klump. Those familiar with the plot of *Carrie* know very well that the story doesn't have a happy ending. Some spilled pig's blood at prom, however, was nothing compared to the horror that was in store for the audience at Riverdale High. Just as she was supposed to step downstage for her big act two solo, the onstage wall rose to reveal Midge Klump dead, impaled with scissors and knives.

According to actor Cody Kearsley, the extras on set the day this scene was taped had no idea what to expect when the curtain rose. Apparently, Midge's bloodied, impaled body looked so realistic that, for the first take, the gasp from the audience was completely authentic!

Her body was surrounded by a message written in blood by the Black Hood threatening that all who had escaped his wrath before would die.

The Black Hood's return deserved a standing ovation, that's for sure, but it was a far cry from what Kevin had envisioned when he dreamed up this production. Instead of roses, folding chairs were flung all over the auditorium as audience members struggled to escape and get home to safety. Sadly, Kevin's directorial debut had not gone exactly as planned, but just like with Julie Taymor and *Spider-Man: Turn Off the Dark*, it would be unfair of us to blame it all on the director.

We can only hope that this does not prevent Kevin from prevailing and giving us more school musicals in the future. Hey, Kevin, if you are looking for two show doctors to come in, you know who to call! We've never been great at arts and crafts, so we can promise no ominous found-letter art coming from us!

After Spider-Man: Turn Off the Dark on Broadway's disastrous early-preview process, producers of the show brought in Riverdale showrunner Roberto Aguirre-Sacasa as a book doctor. They even closed the show for a month to allow Roberto time to completely retool the production. Perhaps this was partly the inspiration behind the Carrie episode.

GUILTY OF

- Cruising in the woods

- Not having Alice Cooper sing "And Eve Was Weak"

CASE FILE #7

HERMIONE LODGE

HEIGHT: 5'4"

AGE: 44

EYES: BROWN

PORTRAYED BY: MARISOL NICHOLS

The only thing that people enjoy more than a star-is-born narrative is a fall-from-grace story, and boy did Hermione Lodge have one for the books. Originally born in Riverdale as Hermione Gomez, she grew up like every other teenager in town, working an after-school job, drinking milkshakes at Pop's, and flirting with the boys in town. And flirt she did! Before she ended up with rich boy Hiram Lodge, her original high school sweetheart was none other than Fred Andrews. While we do not yet know why Fred and Hermione called it quits, Hermione certainly did not draw the short straw.

Hermione's mother worked grueling hours as a maid at the Five Seasons and barely scraped by. The one thing that Hermione knew for sure was that this was not the sort of lifestyle that she wanted for herself. She had to escape. And although her mother wrote off Hiram as being a petty criminal, Hermione saw something else in him. She saw her ticket to the American dream. So long, milkshakes and burgers, and hello, cocktails and caviar. Hermione quickly traded *The Riverdale Register* for the style section of *The New York Times*. And for a while, she and Hiram lived a fairy-tale life together in New York City.

Though it's never discussed on the show, we like to imagine that before moving back to Riverdale, Hermione was being considered as a cast member for *The Real Housewives of New York City*. We mean . . . she would be *perfect*! Bravo *loves* a crime-centric story line. (Looking at you, Teresa and Joe!) And it would explain the appearance of Andy Cohen when Hermione is running

for mayor. Strangely enough, we could see Hermione getting along well with Bethenny Frankel. They are both strong women who are experts in the art of manipulation. Ramona Singer, however, would be another story. Hermione is a woman who showed no remorse in forcing the entire Southside community out of their homes simply for her own financial gain. This is not the action of a woman who supports other women. Hey, even Countess Luann would have an easy in for a cabaret night at La Bonne Nuit. Although this never came to fruition, perhaps after his visit to town, Andy Cohen might consider adding another city to the franchise with *The Real Housewives of Riverdale*. Personally speaking, we think that Hermione, Penelope, Alice, and Sierra definitely have the makings of an incredible cast!

Of course, as Fantasia Barrino's book, later turned original Lifetime movie, has taught us, life is not a fairy tale. Hiram's sentence devastated Hermione. We would have to imagine that her mother's words of warning echoed through Hermione's head as Hiram was carted off to prison. Yet, as history has proved time and time again, behind every powerful man is an even more powerful woman pulling the strings. Yes, staying in Manhattan and being subject to all the backstabbing gossip among the social elite sounds anything but pleasant. But did Hermione Lodge move back to her hometown of Riverdale with a larger goal in mind? One thing was for certain: Hermione was no innocent puppet in Hiram Lodge's master plan.

Hermione is as shady as they come. As if it was not bad enough that she hurt Fred Andrews by leaving him for rich boy Hiram Lodge when they were in high school, as soon as Hermione returned to town, she took advantage of Fred once again. While she played the role of struggling wife who was in need of a job quite well, it soon became very clear that Hermione had other motives in becoming a part of Andrews Construction. She needed Fred's help in securing land and building up her and Hiram's SoDale project.

Fred was not the only Andrews boy she managed to take control of. Let's not forget the time when she hired a man to pretend to be an FBI agent to intimidate Archie into snitching about the secrets of the Lodge family. We don't know whether we should be relieved or worried that Archie passed this test with flying colors. He managed to keep his promise of complete loyalty to the Lodge family, and in return he was rewarded by "the boss" by being welcomed as an official family member. In that moment, we learned that the true boss of the Lodge empire is not, in fact, Hiram but rather Hermione.

Remember when Hermione briefly returned to her job at Pop's? Imagine if all her former Upper East Side friends had seen that!

The full scale of the Lodges' plan for Riverdale remains to be seen. With their development of the SoDale project and their acquisition of almost every property in town, the Lodge family is clearly up to something more devious than buying vacation homes.

Even their plan for a for-profit prison seems slightly small potatoes compared to the work that they have put into taking control of the town.

With Hermione now mayor of the town, there is no limit to the power that she and Hiram hold over Riverdale. Buckle up, folks, because this is one power couple we would not want to get on the wrong side of.

GUILTY OF

- Being involved in very shady business dealings

- Being the wife of a mob boss and sometimes serving as the mob queen

- Extortion

- Not making Andy Cohen her second-in-command when appointed mayor

CASE FILE #8

HIRAM LODGE

HEIGHT: 5'8"

AGE: 47

EYES: BROWN

PORTRAYED BY: MARK CONSUELOS

As children we fear the monsters under our bed. We picture them emerging from the floorboards as giant beasts who have come to haunt us. Slowly we grow older and our imagination gets smaller. The monsters, however, do not. They just appear in different forms and wear different uniforms. Hiram Lodge exists as proof that there is no scarier monster than a businessman in a suit.

Hiram is CEO of Lodge Industries and a ruthless tycoon. When the series began, he had just been sent to the Yonkers Penitentiary for multiple counts of fraud and embezzlement. Yet prison time did not stop him from working. His arrest sent his wife and daughter scrambling out of Manhattan to his small hometown of Riverdale, and it would prove to be the perfect opportunity to take over the town that raised him. In Manhattan, Hiram was just one of many evil businessmen. In Riverdale, however, he could have control of the entire town himself. He had been witness to how well Clifford Blossom had been able to do for himself with his drug running and wanted in on it. Riverdale may be a small town, but Hiram saw the possibility of big money.

From prison he anonymously started buying up properties in town, including the Twilight Drive-In, Pop's, Southside High, and the Whyte Wyrm. With Hermione's help, he was able to get Andrews Construction on board but he still had the wherewithal to send thugs to trash the construction site when word of Hermione and

Hello, *American Psycho* much?! One time Ryan went on a couple of dates with this guy whose dating profile was exclusively quotes from the *American Psycho* movie. Having never seen the movie, Ryan did not realize that this was the case until he saw *American Psycho: The Musical*, written by none other than Roberto Aguirre-Sacasa. Needless to say, he quickly called off the relationship. It seemed like a red flag.

Fred's affair reached him. There was even a moment in time when we suspected that he could have had Jason Blossom killed from prison. At the annual banquet for the board of Blossom Maple Farms, Archie overheard Clifford Blossom telling Penelope that it was he who was responsible for locking up Hiram Lodge! This certainly seems like plenty of motive for Hiram to have sought revenge by killing Jason.

Once the dust from Jason's murder had settled and Hiram was released from prison, it seemed as though everything was perfectly laid out for him to complete his vision. Clifford Blossom was dead, and now Hiram could be the town's ruler. Sure, there were also multiple men dressed as serial killers on the loose, but that was something that Hiram could take advantage of. The chaos that the Black Hood's reign created in the town was the perfect opportunity for Hiram to come in and seize control. Talk about kicking a dog while it's down!

We love a fireplace moment. It is kept fairly chilly on set, so the thought of snuggling up near a fireplace is a rather enticing idea.

By using the optics that the Southsiders were responsible for the uptick of crime in town, Hiram was able to sway public opinion to the point of agreeing with him when he wanted to evict them all from their homes. He also knew that he could take advantage of Archie by making him believe that he was the town hero who could save them all from the Black Hood. The Red Circle vigilante group that Hiram persuaded him to start both distracted Archie from his daughter and made Fred Andrews look like a bad candidate for mayoral office. The Black Hood shootings could not have been better for Hiram if he had planned them himself—so did he?

One thing that we kept asking ourselves was what was Hiram Lodge's ultimate plan for Riverdale, anyway? Buying *The Riverdale Register* from the Coopers made sense in that it meant he held complete control over the press in town. But what good does purchasing Pop's Chock'lit Shoppe and the Twilight Drive-In do? Yes, the idea of endless burgers is tempting, but judging by Hiram's well-cut suits, it did not seem as though it was burgers he was after. We then learned that Hiram Lodge was not, in fact, trying to rid Riverdale of crime. Instead, he was looking to bring more crime to Riverdale by turning Southside High into a private, for-profit prison and housing its workers in SoDale.

Hiram's bar setup.

We have a suspicion that Hiram is after far more than just a prison. Hiram seems pretty intent on making Archie's life a living hell. First he framed Archie for murder, and then he organized prison riots and oversaw the implementation of an in-prison fight club. We know that it was Hiram who first introduced Fizzle Rocks into the game of Gryphons and Gargoyles. Could he be the Gargoyle King behind all the chaos in town? So far, dads in this town do not have a great track record. In fact, we are almost running out of fathers to sentence for murder. With the Southside in his grasp and his band of cronies firmly on his side, what is to stop him from taking over the north side as well? Watch out, Riverdale. Hiram has not come to play.

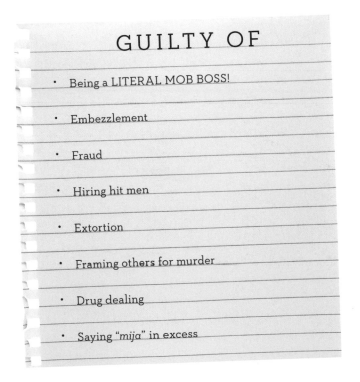

GUILTY OF

- Being a LITERAL MOB BOSS!

- Embezzlement

- Fraud

- Hiring hit men

- Extortion

- Framing others for murder

- Drug dealing

- Saying "mija" in excess

JOSIE McCOY

HEIGHT: 5'3"

AGE: 17

EYES: BROWN

PORTRAYED BY: ASHLEIGH MURRAY

W hat was Beyoncé like in high school? Look no further than Miss Josephine McCoy, Riverdale's resident diva.

Named after the iconic Josephine Baker, Josie was born with music in her blood. Her father, Myles McCoy, is a professional jazz musician, constantly on the road performing all over the world. Because of this, Josie was raised primarily by her mother, Sierra McCoy, who, for the majority of Josie's young life, was the mayor of Riverdale. With such busy parents, Josie was left to fend for herself growing up. It was this need for self-sufficiency that led her to be the spunky, ambitious, confident teen we know and love. Of course, Josie is probably most well-known for her band, Josie and the Pussycats.

With Josie on lead vocals and guitar, she recruited classmates Valerie and Melody into the band, donning signature cat ears way before Ariana Grande made them cool. Together, the Pussycats worked hard, practicing each day after school and writing original songs. They also mastered the art of covering cult favorites such as Kelis's power anthem "Milkshake" and the hit song "Out Tonight" from the musical *Rent*.

Just as happens in practically every music group throughout history, Josie soon had the epiphany that she needed to go solo. The Kelly and Michelle to her Beyoncé were proving to be unnecessary, and Josie secretly started working on writing songs of her own. Let's just say that

When we were growing up, there were a few people in our respective high schools who had bands, but they would only do grungy emo songs. If we'd had a group like Josie and the Pussycats at our schools, it would have been a total game changer.

Melody and Valerie did not take this news well. It was all very similar to the "It's All Over" sequence from *Dreamgirls*. They couldn't believe that after all their time together, Josie would leave them high and dry. How would the band possibly go on? Granted, the Spice Girls are currently touring without Posh, but something feels wrong about Josie and the Pussycats touring without Josie. For the time being, the group has had to make do with Veronica taking lead vocals. Maybe it's just us, but Veronica and the Pussycats doesn't have the same ring to it.

Aside from her band, Josie is also a member of the River Vixens, and she is one of the sole individuals at Riverdale High whom Cheryl Blossom is nice to—perhaps too nice. Before Toni Topaz transferred to Riverdale High, it was Josie McCoy who was the object of much of Cheryl Blossom's affection, and she went to great lengths to prove it. She even went so far as to send a pig's heart to Josie with a note attached reading, "If I can't have you, no one can." Yes, in the past we have gone to great lengths to win over guys, but even we can acknowledge that this crosses a line.

Flashback to the time Sam "accidentally" kept showing up to her crush's workout class even though she had a deep resentment about group exercise and also happens to be physically inept.

It remains to be seen how successful Josie's solo career will be, but we have to allow her the time to grow. Let's not forget that when Beyoncé released her first solo album, *The New York Times* reviewed it by simply saying that she was "no Ashanti." Thankfully, Veronica has offered Josie a permanent residency as the headliner at La

Bonne Nuit. First the basement of a Riverdale diner; next stop, the world! Laser-focused on her road to stardom, Josie tends to remain innocent about the town's crimes. But her former kitty cats remain bitter. Valerie and Melody have been suspiciously absent throughout the town's darkest days. Could they be behind some of the dark goings-on in town? The motive is there—what's a scorned band to do without their star? Only time will tell.

GUILTY OF

- Leaving her band to go solo. RIP, sisterhood.

SIERRA McCOY

HEIGHT: 5'5"

AGE: 47

EYES: BROWN

PORTRAYED BY: ROBIN GIVENS

The spirit of Riverdale flows through Sierra McCoy's veins. Born and raised in town, she learned from an early age that to effect change globally, you must start locally. In many ways she seemed destined for a life in public service. Even in high school she was a staunch anti-apartheid activist. And while her former husband, Myles, was often on the road performing, Sierra knew that Riverdale was the place for her to be. Like so many of her feminist heroes, she wanted to make history, and for a good stretch of time, she served as an excellent mayor of Riverdale. Well, excellent until she started to turn corrupt. It's incredible how easily things can go downhill when a town is in crisis.

It cannot be easy being the mayor of Riverdale. When Sierra first took the job, she most likely figured that her days would be spent dealing with allocating taxpayer money and maybe proposing adding a bike lane to the center of town. Little did she know that she would eventually be dealing with murders, a serial killer, and a live-action role-playing game gone terribly wrong! Not only was she having to contend with that crime, she also then had the Lodges breathing down her neck.

With the Lodges, absolutely nothing is off-limits when it comes to getting what they want, including Sierra's personal life. We all know that a career in politics is an open invitation into every aspect of your life, both professionally and personally.

When Sierra won the election, she was subjected to many people's very vocal opinions questioning her choices and giving her

The two of us could NEVER run for any sort of office with the number of skeletons we have lying around in our closets.

flak. She navigated this with the dignity of a queen, all the while raising her daughter to be strong and independent, much like Sierra herself.

While Sierra was riding a high of professional success, her marriage had taken a bit of a backseat. Due to his travel-heavy career, Myles was rarely in Riverdale. On those rare instances when he was home, he was exhausted and shut off. We've seen this time and again. Some men just can't handle a more successful ←⟍ woman.

We're looking at you, Jason Hoppy.

It's a fact that no matter how self-actualized a woman is, love has a sneaky way of creeping up behind her and slapping her in the face. For Sierra McCoy, love found her again when she wasn't even looking. And while she was still married. #SCANDALOUS!

As mayor, Sierra often crossed paths with Sheriff Keller. The two had an easy kinship. Both had absentee partners and were essentially raising their children as single parents. We'd like to imagine it began innocently one night while the two were both working late. Perhaps they ordered takeout from Pop's, lit a maple-scented candle, and . . . you know the rest. Affairs are tricky situations, but Sierra and Tom seem to be the real deal. Their friendship turned to love, and honestly, who could deny people happiness like that? Answer: the Lodges.

Sierra McCoy's mayorship was an obstacle for Hiram Lodge. He needed her out in order to accelerate his plans for the Southside. After Veronica warned Sierra of her parents' plan to expose her affair, she chose to resign. She would go back to her legal career and spend more time with Josie. This was not an easy decision to make, but in the moment, it seemed like the right one. Going back to her roots will be good for the town—especially at a time when so many of Riverdale's own need a strong bulldog of a lawyer beside them. Sierra has already represented Fangs Fogarty, Veronica Lodge, and even Archie Andrews. With this town's track record, Sierra will be defending Riverdale until the day she dies. Which hopefully isn't any time soon. She is a newlywed, after all!

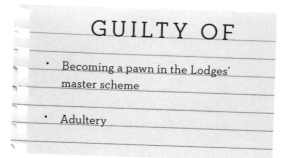

GUILTY OF

- Becoming a pawn in the Lodges' master scheme

- Adultery

CASE FILE #11

TOM KELLER

HEIGHT: 5'9"

AGE: 48

EYES: GREEN

PORTRAYED BY: MARTIN CUMMINS

Poor Tom Keller has a lot on his plate. We are sure that when he became sheriff, he had no idea of the amount of turmoil that would soon strike Riverdale. When taking the position of a police officer in a small, sleepy town like Riverdale, you assume that you will mostly be dealing with parking tickets and the occasional family dispute. As Tom Keller soon learned, however, the family disputes in this town were far greater than just heated Thanksgiving dinner conversations.

Perhaps this is why Sheriff Keller is so bad at his job. No shade toward Tom Keller—he seems like a lovely gentleman and is certainly easy on the eyes. But you have to admit that it is embarrassing that time after time, it is left up to a gang of teenagers who are barely receiving a high school education to solve the crimes that are plaguing the town. In fact, the members of the Riverdale police department are so bad at their jobs that for a while we had to sincerely question whether Tom Keller was the man behind the murders. Surely the Black Hood killings had to be an inside job if it was taking that long for the police force to find the culprit.

The one thing that does warm our hearts about Tom Keller, other than his abs, is the way that he treats his son, Kevin. The love that he has for Kevin is unconditional, and we are super into the fact that this series does not highlight any parental struggle over Kevin's sexuality. Just like his classmates at Riverdale High,

We can admit that neither of us have any actual idea how criminal investigations work outside of the Mary-Kate and Ashley movies that we watched growing up, but we imagine that once it becomes clear that you are dealing with a serial killer, you would call a federal agency to come help your investigation. Forget Agent Adams! Can we get some actual help in this town?

Kevin is loved and accepted for who he is, and we have to give a great amount of credit to Tom Keller for raising his son so openly. How many fathers hand their sons car keys and tell them not to go out into the woods cruising? It is truly inspiring that Tom Keller's concern in this situation is not his son having anonymous gay sex in the woods but rather the fact that there is a murderer on the loose who could be lurking among those having gay sex in the woods.

We love a sex-positive dad! Sure, it would be slightly hypocritical for him to not be this way, as Tom Keller himself got wrapped up in an extramarital affair with Mayor McCoy. With their close working relationship and their distant relationships with their respective spouses, there was bound to be some sort of spark between the two. But who could have imagined that wedding bells were in their future? Nothing bonds people closer together than a common enemy. With Hiram Lodge having removed both of them from their prior positions, it makes sense that they would join forces.

Perhaps without the bureaucracy of the local government, Tom Keller may actually be able to get more accomplished. Heaven knows the town is going to need him. With Hiram holding so much power, Riverdale will need its more virtuous citizens to step up to the plate and fight for what the town truly stands for.

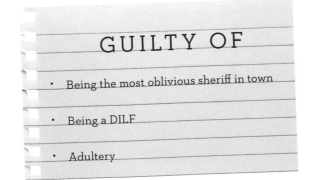

GUILTY OF

- Being the most oblivious sheriff in town
- Being a DILF
- Adultery

TONI TOPAZ

HEIGHT: 5'3"

AGE: 17

EYES: BROWN

PORTRAYED BY: VANESSA MORGAN

Antoinette "Toni" Topaz was born and raised in Riverdale's Southside. A pink-haired firecracker with a penchant for photography, Toni is as cool as it gets. Growing up on the Southside, Toni worked hard to make ends meet. She followed her parents into the Serpents, doing the Serpent Dance at the age of thirteen and working after school as a bartender at the Whyte Wyrm. Gifted a camera for her Serpent initiation, Toni has a keen eye for capturing the world as she sees it.

Toni's best quality is her loyalty. She has a way of seeing the best in people and sticking by them despite their obvious flaws. When Jughead Jones transferred to the Southside, Toni instantly befriended him and was kind to him, even when he was hesitant about whether to officially join the Serpents. After a brief flirtation between the two, they remained friends when the sparks fizzled. When the two ended up back at Riverdale High, Jughead asked her to be *The Blue and Gold*'s official photographer, much to Betty's dismay.

Fortunately, Betty's jealousy was short-lived as Toni quickly set her sights on none other than Cheryl Blossom. As Maureen in *Rent* once said, "Boys, girls, I can't help it, baby!" Toni Topaz and Cheryl Blossom are officially one of our favorite couples. Toni calms Cheryl, while Cheryl spices Toni up. It's the perfect yin and yang. #Choni forever.

Although Toni's head seems to be in the right place, she's a Southsider at heart. We're cautiously optimistic that she will remain loyal to those who do right by her, but we do feel she could somehow be influenced by Hiram and his goons. With Toni's tough upbringing, it would be understandable if she turned on the people she loves for the promise of a better life. Who could blame her? Listen—if Hiram gave us a six-figure check to do some questionable tasks for him, we would say yes in a heartbeat. It's a tough world out there!

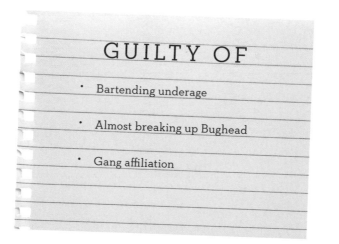

GUILTY OF

- Bartending underage

- Almost breaking up Bughead

- Gang affiliation

CASE FILE #13

NICK ST. CLAIR

HEIGHT: 5'9"

AGE: 17

EYES: BLUE

PORTRAYED BY: GRAHAM PHILLIPS

I t's a well-known fact that children born and bred in Manhattan's Upper East Side grow up five times faster than kids anywhere else. At age seven they're ordering *omakase*, by fourteen they're on every VIP guest list, and by sixteen they have finished their first stint in rehab. *Gossip Girl* didn't lie.

Children of the Upper East Side are born into a specific breed of royalty. Parents pass the diamond-encrusted baton of privilege down to their spawn, who are then put in charge of keeping the power and staying on top of the world.

Xander and Simone St. Clair are a prominent couple within Manhattan social circles. With a brownstone in Carnegie Hill, a summer home in Southampton, and a calendar filled with benefits at Sotheby's and Cipriani, they live the New York City dream. Simone came from old real estate money, and Xander made his fortune in the music industry, where he currently owns a major label. But their biggest investment was their son, Nicholas St. Clair. All his life, Nick had been groomed to take over the family empire.

Like so many private school boys, Nick excels in the art of deceit. Devilishly handsome, Nick is a smooth talker and a real charmer. His people-pleasing demeanor gives him access to everything. And because, as a rite of passage, all kids in New York have a therapist or psychopharmacologist, he has the world at his fingertips.

Nick and Veronica met, as so many young New Yorkers do, at a table at 1 OAK freshman year of high school. They bonded instantly and spent their time clubbing, partying, and making the kinds of bad decisions that result in the best stories. Throughout high school, Veronica and Nick were the will-they-or-won't-they couple of the crew—flirting over bathroom bumps, bright pills, and shots of Grey

Goose night after night. The blurriness of those nights bonded them in a way that only kids who grew up with a mastery of avoiding Page Six can; best friends in a perpetual "It's Complicated" Facebook relationship status.

Veronica's relocation to Riverdale created a wedge in the group. Encouraged by his parents, Nick took the last semester off to "rest and reset" at a twenty-thousand-dollar-a-month rehab in Malibu. He emerged from California a budding music producer eager to quickly reunite with his old demons.

When Hiram first invited the St. Clairs to Riverdale, Veronica was thrilled at the thought of seeing her old pal. Ever the businessman, Hiram encouraged his daughter to make sure that Nick was well entertained. If Nick St. Clair was happy, he would get Xander to invest in SoDale. Simple as that.

Veronica swiftly turned on the charm and transformed herself into Daddy's little corporate concierge. As soon as she greeted the St. Clairs at the Five Seasons, Nick instantly remembered just how much of a spell Veronica Lodge had cast on him. Who says that the charmer can't be charmed?

Unfortunately, as we've learned time after time, spells are cast only to be broken. Later that night, Nick held a private party in his hotel room as an opportunity to meet some of the local Riverdale teens. It was as if he were on a safari in Africa and wanted to witness for himself firsthand the small-town simpletons of Riverdale.

What Nick failed to realize, however, was that Riverdale was no longer the serene safe haven that it had once been, and by adding his newly purchased stash of Jingle Jangle to the mix, he was simply pouring gasoline on fire.

While everyone's mind at the Five Seasons raced with the rush of the JJ, Nick St. Clair attempted to respark the flame that he and Veronica had once had. Veronica protested, and Nick insisted, baffled by her resistance.

Dismayed by Veronica's dismissal of him, our visiting sexual predator set his sights on the vulnerable Cheryl Blossom, this time with the aid of a date-rape drug. Thankfully, the Pussycats and Veronica caught wind of his despicable plan and immediately rushed to Cheryl's side. Nick may have been in his fair share of fights before, but he had never met the Pussycats. It turned out the only things sharper than their stilettos were their claws.

It would seem as though Nick St. Clair would have cut all ties with the residents of Riverdale after everything that happened. However, sins have a way of haunting people in this town, and Nick was no exception. On the way back to Manhattan, the St. Clair family was run off the road in a terrible car crash. Make no mistake, though, this was no accident; this was the work of Hiram Lodge.

The car crash wouldn't be the last time that Nick dealt with the repercussions of his actions in town. Upon learning of Nick taking advantage of Veronica, Archie Andrews paid him a visit while he was recovering in the ER, where he beat Nick up. Now, if all of this doesn't give Mr. St. Clair a motive to eventually seek revenge on Riverdale and all the teens in it, we don't know what does. He definitely has a little sociopath in him, as many NYC private school students do. Let's just say Nick St. Clair is a shady character who might not be done with Riverdale yet. Some monsters wear hoods, and others carry Amex Black Cards.

GUILTY OF

- Sexual assault
- Date rape
- Purchasing drugs
- Still being a boy Sam and Ryan would definitely fall in love with

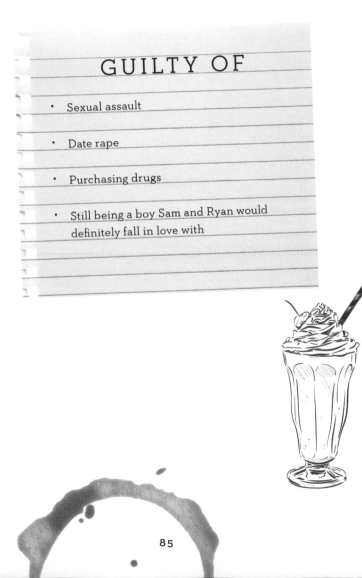

FRED ANDREWS

HEIGHT: 5'10"

AGE: 48

EYES: BROWN

PORTRAYED BY: LUKE PERRY

F red Andrews is your classic, old-fashioned American dad! Father to Archie and owner of Andrews Construction, he is just trying to live the American dream of owning his own small business, providing for his family, and occasionally catching a football game or two. Okay, so he may also flirt with Hermione Lodge from time to time, but you have to forgive him. With a beard like Luke Perry's, you'd have us saying "9021-hello, which way to the bedroom?" too.

If there is anything that the town of Riverdale cherishes, it is tradition, and the Andrews family is no exception to this rule. For all

The Andrewses' back porch! Here you can see one of the drops used to make it look as though this is a real backyard. Wonder when that croquet set was last used.

of Archie Andrews's life, he seemed groomed to follow the same path as his father. It seemed like destiny that Archie would grow up to become the high school football hero and eventually go on to take over the family construction business.

Fred Andrews's current reading material. He's just trying to be the best dad he can be!

Over the summer before sophomore year, however, our Home Depot hunk found a new passion for songwriting. He spent countless late nights quietly practicing his guitar and writing out lyrics on pieces of scrap paper in his room. Fred Andrews, while a major champion of Archie's dreams, is also a realist and is fiercely protective of his son's future. He could not understand why Archie would give up on his blossoming football career to pursue music.

Now, this is where things get complicated. As two people who grew up involved in the arts our entire lives, we can personally attest to the power of arts education. Sports have just never made sense to us. Ryan tried joining a T-ball team for three weeks, and the coach had to pull his parents aside to explain how his constant knocking down of the tee instead of hitting the ball was holding back the other players. Yet we can sympathize with Fred Andrews here as well. There are few things more insufferable than having to listen to a child practice an instrument before they have fully mastered it. Fred Andrews's creating that soundproof music room in his garage seemed like it was a benevolent gesture toward his son, but in reality, he was just trying to save his own sanity. And for that we respect you, Fred.

There is a whole lot to respect about Fred Andrews. In fact, he most likely would have had our vote for mayor of Riverdale. It was even more of a surprise, then, when Fred Andrews became the prime target for the Black Hood. While this thankfully clears his name of any sort of personal foul play, inevitably you have to ask why the Black Hood would be so insistent on killing Fred. Could he possibly be hiding something much more sinister behind those killer (no pun intended) brown eyes?

Who could possibly have a vendetta against Fred Andrews? Oh, that's right! Remember when we mentioned that he was having an affair with the wife of a convicted felon and mobster? Similar to his own son, Fred had managed to find himself entwined with Hiram Lodge, a situation no one in their right mind wants to be in.

This is just one of the many staircases on set that lead to . . . nowhere.

With his construction company hemorrhaging money, winning the bid for the SoDale projects was the only way to keep all his workers employed. If this meant dealing with an unknown buyer, then so be it. It was not until much later down the road that Fred learned that Hermione and Hiram were the anonymous buyers and that he had been working for Lodge Industries the entire time.

From prison, Hiram Lodge had turned Fred Andrews into his own personal puppet, and as soon as Hiram was released, he no longer had a use for Fred. (Well, besides the time the Lodges tried to manipulate Fred into running for mayor just to further their agenda.) Suspiciously enough, more often than not, it seemed that throughout the Black Hood's reign, Fred Andrews was the one who found himself staring down the barrel of a gun, whether it be at Pop's, the mayoral debate, or in his own home on the night of Hal Cooper's confession.

That night, as Archie went to lock the doors of his house, he was attacked from behind by yet another man in a black hood. But just like during the town hall and diner shootings from before, it was clear that this killer was not after Archie; he was looking for Fred. As Archie and the shooter wrestled it out on the living room floor, Fred stepped in to help his son, and by doing so, he put himself directly into the line of fire. As soon as the black-hooded killer was able to stand up again, he shot Fred right in the chest and ran off into the night. Miraculously, Fred was unharmed as he was still wearing the bulletproof vest Sheriff Keller had given him when they went to break up a Ghoulies brawl in Pop's parking lot.

This town seems to have more hoods than a Benedictine monastery! With Hal Cooper having already confessed, authorities set out to find this other hood-donning gunman. They discovered that he was none other than FP's former right-hand man, Tall Boy, who, as per orders from Hiram Lodge, had also donned a black hood and targeted Fred. We know that we let Hiram off the hook for almost everything that he does, but the fact that the show has not even addressed that Hiram was the main conspirator in an attempt to murder Fred Andrews does seem glaring.

As Sara Bareilles wrote for her musical *Waitress*, "She is messy, but she tries." This essentially sums up Fred Andrews. He means the best, but he inevitably falters every so often, as we all do.

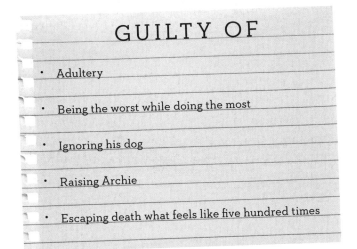

GUILTY OF

- Adultery
- Being the worst while doing the most
- Ignoring his dog
- Raising Archie
- Escaping death what feels like five hundred times

FP JONES

HEIGHT: 5'10"

AGE: 48

EYES: BROWN

PORTRAYED BY: SKEET ULRICH

As the person who has seemingly been convicted of the most crimes in Riverdale, FP Jones sits shockingly low on our list of lead suspects. Yes, he has his rough patches, but don't we all? While he grew up in Riverdale alongside Fred, Penelope, Alice, Hal, Hiram, and Hermione, life at home was never easy for FP. When things took a turn for the worse, he joined the Southside Serpents and created a new family for himself. It was among the Serpents that FP found comfort, but it was also where he began to get dragged down into a life of crime.

Listen, FP is certainly no saint in this story. His aggressive tendencies and abusive relationship with alcohol led to his wife and daughter leaving him. He even allowed his own son, Jughead, to raise himself in the projection booth of a drive-in movie theater.

Did no one else in town find this problematic?

FP's trailer! Crazily enough, it smells exactly how you'd think it does.

And although he attempted to hold a steady job with Fred Andrews at Andrews Construction, he was eventually let go after he was caught stealing from the company. Since the Black Hood specifically targeted Fred Andrews, it would make some sense if FP were behind the shooting at Pop's. But thankfully he had the pretty rock-solid alibi of being locked up in jail for the murder of Jason Blossom. What we're trying to say is, we do love FP, but we are not looking at a father of the year here.

We picture FP chilling here with his record player after his shifts at Pop's.

Although we ultimately learn that FP was not the person who killed Jason Blossom, he was no innocent bystander. Yes, the murder weapon that was placed in his trailer was just a setup, but law enforcement still had good reason to keep him behind bars. You see, a few weeks before Jason staged his disappearance, he had approached FP in need of a getaway car and some quick cash. Together, they worked out a deal in which FP and the Serpents would

FP's kitchen looks like the kitchen of every New York City apartment that we have ever lived in.

Obsessed with the Jones boys' cereal collection.

provide Jason with a car and cash if, in return, Jason delivered a shipment of drugs to another gang in a neighboring town. However, once FP discovered that Jason was Clifford and Penelope Blossom's son, he realized that Jason was worth far more to the Serpents than that one drug deal.

After sending his henchman Mustang to capture Jason and bring him to the Whyte Wyrm, FP tied up Jason and held him for ransom. Sure enough, Clifford Blossom came through with a whopping amount of cash and arrived to collect his son. But instead of taking Jason home, Clifford Blossom shot him and left his body there for the Serpents to take care of.

On the bright side, FP being locked up cleared him of any involvement in the Black Hood shootings. But the fact that he was being charged for dumping a dead kid's body in the river, making a false confession, destruction of evidence, arson, and obstruction of justice was far from ideal. His lawyer at the time suggested that he take the plea deal that he was being offered, for which he could face twenty years in prison. All things considered, that sounds relatively fair to us, but for Jughead this would still be too long without his father. With Betty's help, Jughead convinced Cheryl to publicly forgive FP on behalf of her family in court and explain how FP was threatened by her father to carry out all the crimes that he was being charged with. Miraculously, the court was sympathetic to FP's case and let him off after what felt like only mere weeks.

Once FP left jail, he had planned to put his Southside Serpent past behind him, but with Jughead now tied up in a pact with Penny Peabody and an impending war between the Serpents, Ghoulies, and Northsiders drawing nearer, this was no time to leave his family

In general, we are rather confused with how the prison system works in the *Riverdale* universe. Like Dorothy said, "People come and go so quickly around here." Archie was sent to prison for two years, which is definitely a long time for a crime you did not commit, but two years for murder seems like a rather short sentence. As viewers we are not complaining. As entertaining as an *Orange Is the New Black* spinoff at the Leopold and Loeb detention center might be, there is only so much shirtless fighting that we can watch. And believe us, we can watch a lot of shirtless fighting.

without a leader. He had let his son down one too many times in the past and was not about to let it happen again.

His romantic fling with Alice Cooper now rekindled, FP set out to create a new chapter for himself and the Serpents. Much darker forces were at play within town than a group of leather and motorcycle enthusiasts. With the Ghoulies gaining power and Hiram Lodge's grip growing ever tighter, the Southside needed a leader who could carry them through to safety. Personally speaking, FP could lead us anywhere he wants to.

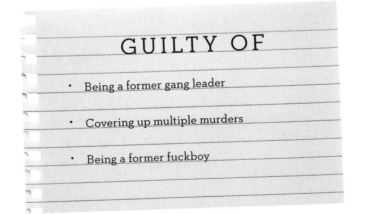

GUILTY OF

- Being a former gang leader

- Covering up multiple murders

- Being a former fuckboy

CASE FILE #16

ALICE COOPER

HEIGHT: 5'6"

AGE: 47

EYES: GREEN

PORTRAYED BY: MÄDCHEN AMICK

At first glance, the Coopers seemed like the perfect all-American family, with two loving parents, a straight-A daughter, and a white picket fence that would make even Martha Stewart jealous. Underneath this facade, however, the family was in absolute turmoil.

Let's focus on Alice Cooper, the matriarch of the Cooper clan. Manipulative, controlling, and vicious, Alice playing Margaret White in *Carrie* was clear typecasting that we were honestly here for.

How does one become this way? Alice was born in Riverdale's Southside and attended Riverdale High. As a rebellious young teen, she became involved with the Southside Serpents and started a relationship with mega-hunk FP Jones. Imagine a young Skeet Ulrich in a leather jacket. Who could blame her?

It should be noted that most of the parents of Riverdale were once major stars of '80s and '90s film and television! Skeet Ulrich was known for playing Billy Loomis in *Scream*, Mädchen Amick for her role as Shelly in the original *Twin Peaks* series, Molly Ringwald for her starring roles in John Hughes films, and Luke Perry for his role as Dylan McKay in *Beverly Hills, 90210*.

During Alice's tenure with the Serpents, one thing was certain: she was a troublemaker. It was revealed through the Black Hood that she was even arrested at one point. And while the details of why she eventually cut all ties with the Serpents remain hazy, perhaps it had something to do with the child she was carrying.

Her pregnancy aligned with both her departure from the Serpents and her breakup with FP Jones. Wasting no time, she immediately started dating Hal Cooper. Hal, a straitlaced, simple, all-American guy, was a safe departure from FP and, for Alice, must have seemed like the better option to raise a child with. But upon learning the news of her pregnancy, Hal pushed Alice to get an abortion, telling her that she was simply unfit to be a mother at the time. And this was before he even knew that the baby was actually FP's. Instead of terminating the pregnancy, Alice pulled a *Juno* and lived with the Sisters of Quiet Mercy until the baby was born. She then left her son there to be adopted and moved on with her life.

And so, the white-picket-fence facade was built. Alice left the Southside, cut ties with the Serpents, married Hal, and had two daughters, Polly and Betty. She and Hal bought the local newspaper, *The Riverdale Register*, and Alice worked tirelessly as editor in chief. But the ghosts of the past have a way of haunting you, no matter how hard you try to keep them at bay. When Polly became pregnant with Jason Blossom's baby, Hal tried hard to get her to terminate the pregnancy. Alice's fury at this changed her and Hal's relationship forever. She kicked him out of the house, and then he went on to casually become a deluded serial killer, as one does.

Drama continued to surround Alice's life when her youngest daughter started dating Jughead Jones. Consumed by her Serpent past and illicit child with FP, Alice was not a fan of this relationship. Her control over Betty began to slip when her daughter started to rebel and become entranced with the Serpents. The apple truly doesn't fall far from the tree.

As if this wasn't enough, Alice's resolve was truly tested when a creepy criminal masquerading as her dead son showed up on her doorstep. Let's not forget that she assisted in the covering up of a murder in her very own living room thanks to Chic. If we were in her shoes we would be running to join the Farm as well!

Despite her icy personality and Norma Bates parenting skills, Alice seems to be at the center of the crime rather than the root of it. At the end of the day, she's just trying to be a good mother, despite her faults.

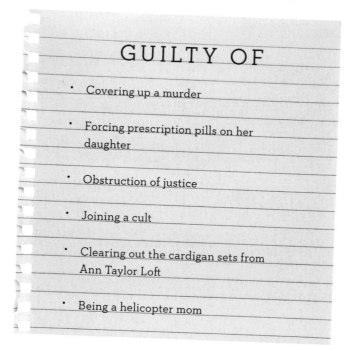

GUILTY OF

- Covering up a murder

- Forcing prescription pills on her daughter

- Obstruction of justice

- Joining a cult

- Clearing out the cardigan sets from Ann Taylor Loft

- Being a helicopter mom

POLLY COOPER

HEIGHT: 5'9"

AGE: 18

EYES: GREEN

PORTRAYED BY: TIERA SKOVBYE

In *Moulin Rouge*, the greatest movie of our time (according to Sam, who went to film school), there is a quote: "The greatest thing you'll ever learn is just to love and be loved in return." No one understands this better than Polly Cooper.

Cheerleader, student, daughter, and sister, Polly was loyal, loving, and kind, with one huge kryptonite—a boy named Jason Blossom.

Due to the long-standing feud between the Blossom and Cooper families, Polly was warned by her parents not to date Jason. But if TLC's *90 Day Fiancé* has taught us anything, it is that love conquers all—even in the face of not understanding a single word your partner utters while being stuck in the Amazon getting mugged by men with machetes. And so, Jason and Polly fell in a deep, true, all-consuming love.

Both families were less than thrilled with their children's tumultuous romance. The Blossom family forced Jason to break up with Polly, pleasing the Coopers. But Polly eventually became pregnant with Jason Blossom's baby. The two became engaged in secret—bound together with Nana Rose's blessing and family ring. Polly and Jason made plans to run away and start a new life. On that fateful July 4th morning, Polly had just packed her bags, ready to meet Jason at Sweetwater River, when her parents intercepted her. They had learned of her plans to run away and sent her to live at the Sisters of Quiet Mercy.

While Polly was with the sisters practicing her Hail Marys, Jason was saying his final prayer. Were Polly and Jason simply Riverdale's Romeo and Juliet, star-crossed lovers who were doomed from the start? Or was there something even darker at play? And, if so, how far would the families go to protect themselves from each other? Before we could find out, Polly knew she had to protect herself.

Upon hearing of the Black Hood's initial killings, Polly left the Cooper house and went to live at "the Farm."

In season three, "the Farm" is proven to DEFINITELY be a cult, à la *Wild Wild Country*.

There, she gave birth to her twins, Juniper and Dagwood. Okay, excuse us, but what kind of names are JUNIPER AND DAGWOOD?! Even Kim Kardashian's children have better names. But we digress. Upon learning of Clifford Blossom's secret will, she returned to Riverdale, not knowing she was to be met with even more sinister secrets . . . including a long-lost brother and the reveal of her murderous father. If we were Polly, we would need a *lot* of therapy. We kind of don't blame her for joining a cult. Let's just hope she doesn't go all Manson Family on us.

GUILTY OF

* Persuading her mother to join a cult

* Naming her children Juniper and Dagwood

* Incest

* Gone *Girl*-ing herself

Remember when the show just totally skirted over the fact that Jason and Polly are technically related?

CHIC COOPER

HEIGHT: 5'11"

AGE: 25

EYES: GREEN

PORTRAYED BY: HART DENTON

I s there anything hotter than a twentysomething sexually fluid master manipulator who steals the identity of his former room-mate whom he murdered to get the family he never had? We think not!

Charles Smith, aka Chic, is the alleged son of Alice and Hal who was given up for adoption many moons ago. After Alice left the Sisters of Quiet Mercy, Chic remained there and was raised by the nuns in what proved to be a very lonely childhood. (Think Maria in *The Sound of Music* but without any hills to escape to.) At age eighteen, without any prospects of finding a Captain who had children that needed to be tended to, he was kicked out and forced to fend for himself.

Flash forward seven years. Alice was devastated by Polly's relocation to "the Farm," so to help lift her spirits, Betty decided to reach out to her long-lost brother. They found him at the Last Resort hostel in Centerville, where he was working in "fantasy fulfillment" as a cam boy. Although Chic was resentful of the Coopers at first, he eventually had a change of heart and moved in with them after his living situation became too dangerous.

While Alice was thrilled to be afforded a second chance to connect with her son, not all of the Coopers were as enthused by their new houseguest. Understandably, Hal was instantly resentful of Chic's presence and urged Alice to kick him out, to no avail. Meanwhile, Betty Cooper was fascinated by the mysterious air that enshrouded her long-lost brother. Although they had never met before, there was clearly something that the two of them seemed to share. In a semisweet moment of sibling bonding, Betty confided to Chic that she hoped he could help reveal why she carries this darkness within her. We would recommend talking about this to a therapist before a weird brother whom you found in a hostel, but you do you, Betty Cooper. In a not-so-shocking turn of events, Chic turns out to be no Dr. Phil. Instead of offering reasonable advice, he merely recommends that Betty also turn to cam-ing as a way to escape reality.

Like Taylor Swift once said, "I knew you were trouble when you walked in." Sure enough, mere weeks into his residency at the Cooper household, Chic turned Alice into a murder accomplice. One night as Alice and Chic sat down for din-

Okay, we know that we are just coming across as broken records, but Betty and Chic bonding over cam-ing was seriously one of the weirdest turns this show has taken. And this is a show entirely built on weird turns! No disrespect meant to sex workers, but does it not seem like the weirdest thing ever to suggest that a sibling do? Maybe we are just old-fashioned.

ner, they were interrupted by a man at the door who was there for Chic. Though details here are murky, Chic allegedly killed him and Alice proceeded to help him cover it up. In a bout of bad timing, Betty was roped into the homicide as well when she walked in the door to find her mother cleaning up blood on their living room floor. They were now all in over their heads. Alice knew that Chic was incredibly damaged and capable of murder, but as any mother would, she tried to pretend that nothing had happened.

Betty soon had to wonder if Chic was even her brother anyway. Growing increasingly suspicious, Betty used the opportunity of the Blossom will reading to test his DNA. Her fears were realized when she learned that Chic had no Blossom blood. Alice again turned a blind eye, telling her daughter this was simply because Hal wasn't Chic's father. Hal, technically, was the one who was a blood relative of the Blossoms. It made sense then that Alice would still feel a maternal connection to Chic and that Hal would want nothing to do with him. But that was still ignoring the fact that they had welcomed a homicidal sex worker into their home. There was more to Chic's story and Betty was determined to get to the bottom of it.

Naturally, Betty enlisted Jughead to help and they returned to the Sisters of Quiet Mercy to dig for evidence that Chic was not who he said he was. Sure enough, they found a picture of the real Charles Smith, who looked nothing like the stranger living in Betty's house. When Betty returned to the house to inform her mother, Chic overheard and attempted to stab Jughead, hurting Alice in the process.

Dark Betty reemerged and tied Chic up in the basement, torturing him (sans sticky maple) for answers. In a dark twist, it was revealed that Chic met the real Charles Smith when they were both living on the streets. They became friendly and moved into the hostel together. Charles often spoke of the family that gave him up and never came back to find him. Although he told Betty that Charles died of a Jingle Jangle overdose, foul play seems more likely. The true story is that Chic wanted the family Charles spoke about, so he learned all he could about the Coopers before killing his roommate and taking on his identity when Alice and Betty knocked.

Dateline wishes it had a story this juicy!

As far as we know, Chic was murdered after Betty delivered him to the Black Hood. However, we never got confirmation or proof of this, and knowing this show he very well may be still at large. If he is, he is incredibly dangerous and might still be out for revenge. We advise you to watch your backs and be careful who you video-chat with.

GUILTY OF

- Murder

- Identity theft

- Drug dealing

- Being REALLY creepy

- Having a dumb name. Chic?! What.

CASE FILE #19

PENELOPE BLOSSOM

HEIGHT: 5'5"

AGE: 47

EYES: BROWN

PORTRAYED BY: NATHALIE BOLTT

What sort of mother is capable of raising a child like Cheryl Blossom? It takes a certain amount of ruthlessness, know-how, and neglect, traits that Penelope Blossom has in spades. Step aside, Adora Crellin; we've got a new mother-of-the-year contender in town. That being said, Penelope is iconic and deserves to be celebrated. She has her downsides, like attempting to kill Nana Rose and sending Cheryl away to conversion therapy, but at the end of the day, she is just a small-business owner attempting to make ends meet.

Her business is the local bordello that she runs out of Thistlehouse. After Clifford hanged himself, Penelope had to start working for the first time to maintain the lifestyle she was used to.

For the truth of the matter is that the Blossoms were broke and with Christmas just around the corner, Penelope chose to take up the world's oldest profession: prostitution.

Penelope had very few options left at this point. While the hush money that she had originally accepted from the St. Clair family

> We never really get an answer about what happened to the Blossom Maple Farms company. We can only imagine that the law would not look kindly on the fact that it was ultimately just a front for transporting drugs, but when Clifford died, who took over the company? When Uncle Claudius arrives in town, Penelope suggests that he take over the company from Nana Rose. But does that mean that the entire empire was hinging on Nana Rose Blossom before this? Perhaps Veronica's involvement in owning a business will inspire Cheryl to take over. Either way, dissolving the business altogether seems like a waste of tapped maple trees.

would have helped for a little bit, even Penelope's cold heart could not take money from a family that had caused so much harm to her daughter. Soon Penelope's clients at Thistlehouse became the who's who of the lonely men of Riverdale, including the Black Hood himself, Hal Cooper.

Is it possible that Hal and Penelope could have been teaming up with ambitions more sinister than just some casual adult playtime?

The one thing that seems certain with Penelope is that she always has some ulterior motive. This fact is never clearer than when Uncle Claudius comes back to town. To-

Yes, we should once again stress that the Blossoms and Coopers are vaguely related. Though we suppose Penelope technically married into the family, so maybe that makes this rendezvous more palatable. We don't make the rules.

gether, they serve us full-out Miss Hannigan and Rooster in *Annie* realness in their attempt to seize control over the Blossom maple syrup empire.

They also both happen to be involved in Hiram Lodge's plan for what he is describing as the New Southside. With the prison soon to be up and operational, Claudius can continue in his brother's footsteps of running drugs through town, but this time with the added protection of the Ghoulies and Hiram Lodge.

At this point, a musical number with Penelope and Claudius performing "Easy Street" around Thistlehouse just seems inevitable.

Poor Penelope has been through a lot. In the span of one year, she has lost her husband and her son; suffered third-degree burns from running into her mansion, which her own daughter set on fire; and has gone from being the wealthiest woman in Riverdale to being a prostitute. Really puts things in perspective when you look at it that way. Yet as bad as things had been, the events surrounding the Southside and the reign of the Gargoyle King seem to be bringing even more darkness into town. Perhaps Penelope Blossom is tired of playing the victim and is ready to raise a little hell herself. One thing is for certain: we would not want to be on the receiving end of Penelope's wrath.

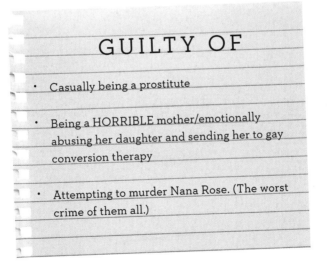

GUILTY OF

- Casually being a prostitute

- Being a HORRIBLE mother/emotionally abusing her daughter and sending her to gay conversion therapy

- Attempting to murder Nana Rose. (The worst crime of them all.)

CASE FILE #20

CLIFFORD BLOSSOM

HEIGHT: 6'0"

AGE: 47

EYES: BLUE

PORTRAYED BY: BARCLAY HOPE

When your entire life centers around the maple syrup industry, things are bound to get sticky. What drove Clifford Blossom to kill his only son and heir to the family business? The best explanation is pride. You see, as a Blossom, you are meant to take pride in your family name. From an early age all Blossoms are taught that business comes first and everything else is second. For Jason to have spit in the face of the family name by attempting to run away was completely unforgivable. Generations of the Blossom family had worked their entire lives to build the empire that they now had. Not only did Jason not want to accept the responsibility of taking over the family business, but he wanted to escape town with a girl who was a member of a rival family. The Blossoms had worked for years to separate themselves from the Coopers. Now here was Jason, joining family blood!

More than that, Jason had discovered the truth behind Blossom Maple Farms. The Blossom empire was not built on a sugary breakfast condiment. Oh no, the sticky truth is that the Blossoms' maple syrup business was simply a front for transporting heroin from Canada. Although Clifford and Penelope attempted to keep this a secret from their children, regaling them with sensational stories of the Sugarman to scare them away from the truth, Jason eventually learned about his father's drug ring and threatened to expose the family secret to the public. For Clifford Blossom, with so much at stake, Jason was better off dead.

After Jason's death, Clifford worked hard to cover his tracks. He had FP Jones and the Serpents put Jason's body into a freezer and keep him at the Whyte Wyrm until the police had done a thorough search of Sweetwater River. He even went so far as to kill Mustang, the Serpent who abducted Jason, and stage it to look like an accidental overdose. Needles were not the only thing that Clifford staged. He also put a bag full of cash from Hiram Lodge in Mustang's hotel room so that suspicion would be cast on Hiram.

Eventually, Clifford could no longer carry the guilt of having killed Jason. Either that or he knew that people in town were onto him and he was unable to face the embarrassment. When Sheriff Keller led his officers up to the Thornhill mansion for Clifford's arrest, they found him hanging by the neck over barrels of his precious maple syrup.

For Clifford, death felt more comfortable than living to see his family name go up in flames. In this case, quite literally. Just a few days after Clifford's suicide, Cheryl Blossom burned Thornhill to a crisp. It was the only way she knew how to begin to cleanse the sins of her family's past.

Fire can destroy, but memories are forever. While the clouds of smoke from Thornhill billowed over the tall trees of Fox Forest, darker powers were at play throughout town. Jason's murderer may have been found, but Clifford Blossom was nothing compared to the upcoming wrath that the town was about to face.

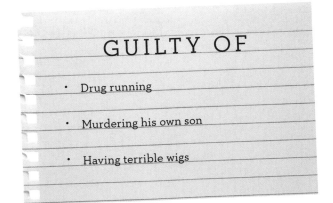

GUILTY OF

- Drug running

- Murdering his own son

- Having terrible wigs

CLAUDIUS BLOSSOM

HEIGHT: 6'0"

AGE: 47

EYES: BLUE

PORTRAYED BY: BARCLAY HOPE

C laudius and Clifford Blossom were both born and raised in Riverdale. Growing up, the two of them were the best of friends and did everything together. However, once it became clear that Claudius was being groomed to inherit the Blossom Maple Farms empire, Clifford grew infuriated. On their fourteenth birthday, Clifford threatened his twin at Sweetwater River. Holding a rifle, he warned him of the Blossom Curse, which stated that it was fate that one twin would meet a violent end at the other's hand. Terrified, Claudius ran away that night and joined the Merchant Marines, convinced that he could outrun the family curse. It was not until Clifford died that Claudius made his grand return to Riverdale, conveniently timed on the day of the reading of Clifford's secret will.

Isn't it funny how family members come crawling out of the woodwork once there is money at stake? ⟵

Claudius's return stunned residents, namely Cheryl Blossom, who, upon seeing a man who was the spitting image of her deceased father, fainted from shock. For you see, Cheryl had no idea her father had a brother, let alone an identical twin! Boy, do we love the zany secrets of the very wealthy. Aside from the lure of the family fortune, Claudius always had a soft spot for Penelope Blossom. When the two reunited at Thistlehouse, they concocted a scheme to remove Nana Rose and Cheryl from the family business and continue Clifford's lucrative side gig involving the town's drug trade.

You know what they say: never trust a man who wears copious amounts of dark turtlenecks. Claudius may not have been in town for long, but he very quickly became a key player in Hiram Lodge's master plan. Along with

Penelope, Penny, Malachai, and Sheriff Minetta, Hiram recruited Claudius to join his motley crew, which he dubbed the New Southside.

> (Begins playing "A New Argentina.") Which reminds us, we would absolutely see a production of Evita starring Mark Consuelos as Che.

There is truly nothing more sinister than a band of evil villains gathered around a shadowy table conspiring. So hide yo' kids, hide yo' wives—something wicked this way comes. This crew is clearly up to no good.

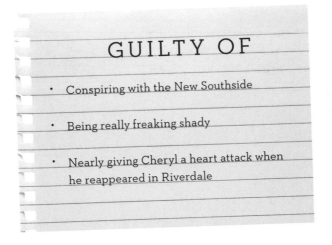

GUILTY OF

- Conspiring with the New Southside
- Being really freaking shady
- Nearly giving Cheryl a heart attack when he reappeared in Riverdale

CASE FILE #22

NANA ROSE

HEIGHT: CURRENTLY
BOUND TO WHEELCHAIR

AGE: VERY OLD

EYES: WHITE AND HAZEL

PORTRAYED BY: BARBARA WALLACE

I f you've ever listened to an episode of *Riverdish*, you know that it is no secret that Ryan's favorite character on *Riverdale* is Nana Rose. From the very first time she rolled her wheelchair into frame, he was obsessed, and a new icon was born.

Roseanne "Rose" Blossom is Clifford and Claudius Blossom's mother and Jason and Cheryl's grandmother. The red streak through her snow-white hair seems to hold more secrets and stories than all the residents of Riverdale combined. Unfortunately, very little is actually known about the early years of Rose Blossom's life.

We would be very into seeing an entire spin-off devoted to exploring Nana Rose's younger days! She herself spent time as a daughter in one of the most important families in Riverdale. What if she had an affair with the Riverdale Reaper (aka Louis Cooper, Betty's grandfather) back in her day? This could potentially explain why she was so sympathetic to the plight of Jason and Polly! All we are saying is, there is a lot of potential here, and we are very much on board to be in the writers' room.

We first met her on the day of Jason Blossom's memorial service at Thornhill. While digging through Jason's bedroom, hungry for any clues that could help uncover Jason's killer, Betty and Jughead were cornered by Nana Rose. Mistaking Betty for Polly, Nana Rose started speaking of a family heirloom ring that she had given Polly. It turns out that Polly and Jason were secretly engaged to be married with the approval of Nana Rose. She not only shared this but also confessed that Great-grandfather Blossom had murdered Great-grandfather Cooper over a dispute regarding their shared maple syrup business.

We suppose now would be a great time to mention that Nana Rose holds some sort of mystical power. Because of course she does! At Polly Cooper's baby shower, Nana Rose performed a ritual on Polly that revealed she was pregnant with twins, a boy and a girl. It was Cheryl who remarked that along with dementia, Nana Rose has Gypsy blood in her.

Yes, we realize that it is a bit silly to keep a crime file on a lady who can barely get to her own breakfast cereal, let alone commit a crime. But we feel it is important to keep a file on her in case she goes missing. Some of the most harrowing months of our lives were those between season one and season two, when we thought that Nana Rose had potentially been killed in the fire that Cheryl set at Thornhill. We must keep Nana Rose alive at all costs! Who knows . . . she may very well be in cahoots with the Gargoyle King.

Actress Barbara Wallace shared with us that for the wrap party of season two, the entire cast and crew received serpents jackets. Nana Rose in leather? We're wet.

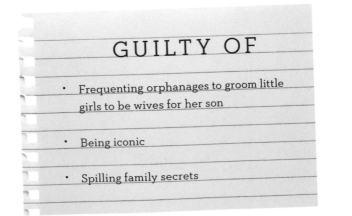

GUILTY OF

- Frequenting orphanages to groom little girls to be wives for her son

- Being iconic

- Spilling family secrets

DILTON DOILEY

HEIGHT: 5'9"

AGE: 17

EYES: BROWN

PORTRAYED BY: MAJOR CURDA

As two former high school drama-department kids, we are in no position to talk about the virtues of popularity. And yet, from the moment we were introduced to Dilton Doiley, we were able to immediately clock him as the leader of the school losers. We hold nothing against him in that regard, but it is clear that we would have very little in common with him if we were students at Riverdale High. In some ways we are jealous of the ingenuity that Dilton must have inevitably acquired as the leader of the local scouts. Just the other night we attempted to hang a poster on a wall, and it resulted in a full-out breakdown involving an iPhone level, a makeshift hammer, and a sore thumb.

Truth be told, we are probably just jealous of Dilton's skills as a DJ. If you don't remember this special skill of Dilton's, you are far from alone but also missing out on a key detail of our character study of him. When a surprise party was being thrown together for Jughead at Archie's house, who was the person who was called? Dilton Doiley, of course. As ABBA would say, "Thank you for the music."

Knowing all this, it came as no surprise to us when Dilton was found dead, having gotten himself too deeply involved in a cult-like game of Gryphons and Gargoyles. Dilton just needed to feel as though he belonged to something larger than himself. It was this desire that led him to become the head scout of the local Riverdale Boy Scout troop and in turn the key witness in the disappearance of Jason Blossom.

On the morning of July 4th, Doiley was allegedly leading his scouts on a bird-watching expedition when they came across a sopping-wet Cheryl Blossom on the river's edge. When initially drilled, Dilton claimed to have not heard the gunshot that was believed to have killed Jason that morning, but Betty and Jughead knew that this had to be a lie. If the scouts were truly watching birds that morning, there would have been no way not to notice the birds flying away in panic after the gunfire.

Of course, after a bit more digging, Betty and Jug eventually learned why Dilton Doiley was playing so coy about the gunshot. For it turned out that it was Dilton Doiley himself who had fired the gun.

As an all-star troop leader, Doiley was a staunch advocate of preparing his troops for anything that might come their way. And although it broke every rule in the Scout handbook, he decided to include handling guns in his curriculum. Frighteningly enough, this was a skill that was presenting itself as being more and more useful in Riverdale.

Terrified that he would be stripped of his troop leader status if news was published of his involvement in teaching his scouts how to handle firearms, Dilton offered *The Blue and Gold* an even juicier story than gunfire. It turns out that Cheryl was not the only familiar sight that he came upon on his morning hike; he had also spotted Ms. Grundy's car.

One thing that is important to note about Dilton Doiley: he's shady as hell. He was willing to sell out Archie and Ms. Grundy just to protect himself from persecution over his firing of guns at Sweetwater River. And while he was not involved directly in the killing of Jason Blossom, he was all too eager to sell a firearm to Archie, who was looking for something to use to protect his father from the Black Hood.

You know those people who always have "a guy" to call for fixing everyday problems? That is Dilton. An everyman who has his hand in everything but is an expert in nothing. He even managed to get himself involved in the short-lived Red Circle. We suppose that having mysterious access to an arsenal comes in handy when throwing together a makeshift militia. Nonetheless, the reality that he was the only non–football player involved in that group was not lost on us.

Now, listen, we realize that it could be considered insensitive to speculate on the criminal activities of someone posthumously. Yet we cannot help but feel as though there still might be more to Dilton's story that has yet to be unveiled. The great Maya Angelou once stated, "When someone shows you who they are, believe them the first time." From the first time we interacted with Dilton, he gave off the vibe of a creepy onlooker who consistently managed to be just on the outskirts of the action. Could our head Boy Scout have had larger motives than teaching survival? Perhaps rather than survival, he was invested in his friend's demise.

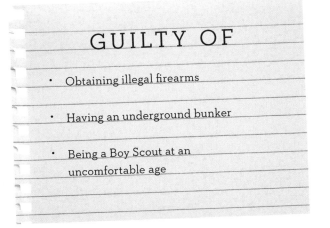

GUILTY OF

- Obtaining illegal firearms

- Having an underground bunker

- Being a Boy Scout at an uncomfortable age

CASE FILE #24

HAL
COOPER

HEIGHT: 6'0"

AGE: 47

EYES: GREEN

PORTRAYED BY: LOCHLYN MUNRO

Where does one even start when trying to unpack Hal Cooper? Buckle up, folks, because Hal's story is a real doozy. Whether we like it or not, we all go around day to day holding on to emotional baggage that we have inherited from family members before us. However, most of us do not deal with this baggage by donning a homemade hood and terrorizing an entire community of people by becoming a serial killer. Does therapy even exist in this town?

The Coopers were originally a part of the Blossom family, making them one of the founding families of Riverdale. (Well, technically the Uktena tribe resided there first, but that is a whole other can of worms.) It seems as though ever since the Blossom brothers tapped their first maple tree, the family has been plagued with more than their fair share of issues. Perhaps calling them "issues" is putting it too lightly. As the brothers' business continued to boom, their respective families became more and more divided, driven by greed and hate. So divided, in fact, that one of the brothers murdered the other and sparked the one side of the family to change their surname to Cooper and forge a new identity in town.

We know that residents in Riverdale have a history of taking games a little too seriously, but the Cooper/Blossom rivalry brought *Family Feud* to a whole new level. And while the Blossoms might be the family that lives in a Gothic mansion and dresses like vampires out of *Twilight*, it is the Coopers who truly carry darkness within them. Yes, Clifford murdering his own son was pretty dark, but it was almost as if Hal felt challenged to one-up the Blossoms with his whole Black Hood scheme. Though what other motive could he have had besides trying to outdo the Blossoms?

The Black Hood made his first attack at Pop's the morning after Betty Cooper's speech at the town jubilee. Betty's speech had shone light on the murky underbelly of the town, but rather than heed her call for peace, Hal interpreted her words as permission to systematically remove all sinners from the town. His first victim was the adulterer Fred Andrews.

We realize that Fred did have a fling with Hermione while she was still married to Hiram, but in the grand scheme of things, he seems like a strange person to make your first target. Fred was not even the married one in that equation. If your priority is wiping out sinners, it would seem as though there were people in town far more guilty than Fred. But we digress.

Miraculously Fred survived, but the Black Hood was far from finished. Just one night later, in the sleepy little town of Greendale, Geraldine Grundy (aka Jennifer Gibson) was up to her old tricks.

After kissing one of her tutoring students, Ben, good night, she went back to her piano bench to tidy up a bit.

Unfortunately for Ms. Grundy, her sonata came to an unexpected conclusion. The man in the black hood had struck again, this time with the cello bow gifted to Geraldine by Archie.

Soon after that, Midge Klump approached Reggie Mantle to score some Jingle Jangle for a special date night with Moose. After successfully obtaining some, Midge and Moose drove their car deep into Fox Forest to try it out. Little did they know that the only elevated heart rate they would be experiencing would be from the fear that would strike them when they were also attacked by the Black Hood.

In the span of just a few days, the Black Hood had attempted

In Netflix's *Chilling Adventures of Sabrina*, Ben Button makes a cameo as a pizza delivery boy at Ms. Wardwell's house! We have so many questions! This delivery must have taken place before he threw himself out of a hospital window because of the Gargoyle King, unless he can somehow magically exist after death in Greendale. (Honestly, nothing would surprise us at this point.) Also, does he live in Riverdale and just travel to Greendale frequently for pizza deliveries and piano lessons? Does he not still work at the Bijou, the local Riverdale movie theater? We demand a spin-off about this Benjamin Button. (And preferably one that doesn't involve Brad Pitt.) Power to him, though, for holding down two jobs in high school and still managing to have time to get fully invested in his game of Gryphons and Gargoyles.

to kill an adulterer, a child molester, and two drug users. Granted, he only actually killed one of them, which does make the Black Hood a laughably bad serial killer. Yet what Hal lacks in murdering skills, he appears to make up for in negotiating prowess. Soon, the Black Hood began making regular phone calls to Betty, convincing her to do his bidding and threatening that if she did not obey, he would murder all her loved ones.

The parent|child relationships on this show are seriously messed up! Imagine receiving these calls from your own father.

Perhaps this was similar to the way in which Hal convinced poor Joseph Svenson, the school janitor, to pretend to be the Black Hood.

For a while the death of Joseph Svenson had seemed to mark the end of terror in Riverdale. The truth of the matter, however, is that Joseph Svenson's death was simply more innocent blood on the town's hands. Hal Cooper had convinced Joseph to wear a black hood and threaten Archie and Betty. This of course led to him getting shot by Sheriff Keller on a bridge over Sweetwater River, and while the rest of the town slept a good night's sleep for the first time in ages, Archie Andrews knew something was wrong. He had seen the eyes of the man who attempted to kill his father, and they did not match those of Mr. Svenson.

Sure enough, the Black Hood made his grand return on the night of the school musical, murdering Midge Klump in plain sight and sending the town back into panic mode. Joseph Svenson was just a red herring, and the real Black Hood was still at large. Once again, neighbors became suspects and family members became foes as the town struggled to figure out who this killer could be. One town member, Betty Cooper, had a suspicion that she was closing in on her target.

The truth was finally revealed one fateful night when the Black Hood visited Cheryl at Thistlehouse. Thankfully, due to Cheryl's expert archery skills, she was able to wound the Black Hood and thwart his attack.

Ryan would like to take this time to apologize to his middle school gym teacher, whom he yelled at during his class's archery unit. Turns out that archery can, in fact, be useful and is not "a complete waste of time," as he suggested back then.

Shortly after Cheryl's call to Betty informing her of what happened, Betty received a phone call from FP letting her know that Hal was in the hospital, wounded. However, by the time Betty finally reached the hospital, her father had already made his escape, leaving in his place a now dead Dr. Masters. It was then that she heard that ominous "Lollipop" ringtone. The Black Hood wanted her home. And he wanted her home now.

When Betty arrived home, her father, still visibly injured, gathered both herself and Alice together for a viewing of some of his old home videos from when he was a young boy. Instead of a charming reminder of simpler times, the video that Hal proceeded to play was scarier than any horror movie ever shown at the Bijou. It showed a young Hal being instructed by his mother to manipulate a young Joseph Svenson (then-Conway) into lying about who it was that killed his family in order to protect Hal's father, who, it turns out, was the real Riverdale Reaper.

Hal also revealed that, contrary to Riverdale lore, it was not Great-grandfather Blossom who killed his brother but rather the other way around. He confessed that there was a darkness that had run throughout the Cooper family for generations. First Great-grandpappy Cooper, then Hal's father, then Hal, and now Betty.

Hal felt an obligation to continue his family legacy of ridding the town of sinners. Yes, through doing so they became sinners themselves, but the sense of superiority felt by the Cooper clan outweighed any moral qualms they had about killing others.

It seemed as though the mystery had been solved. Hal copped to being the Black Hood and agreed to turn himself in. And while the damage that he had caused to his family would be irreparable, there was hope that the Coopers could potentially begin a new chapter with less darkness.

Personally, we cannot help but wonder whether Hal might be one of Hiram's first residents in his Southside prison! We are sure there are vacancies!

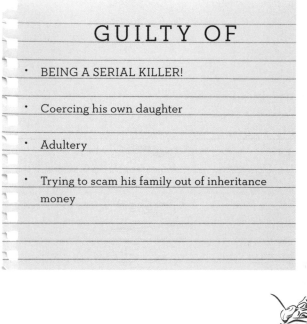

GUILTY OF

- BEING A SERIAL KILLER!

- Coercing his own daughter

- Adultery

- Trying to scam his family out of inheritance money

THE VERDICTS

While we would love to say that we were able to reach a clear verdict regarding the crimes in Riverdale, our report is currently inconclusive. When practically every character in town is guilty of some sort of crime, it becomes impossible to pin down one prime suspect. Yes, some are guiltier than others, but who are we to decide what crimes are the worst? Though we have to believe that it is going to be pretty hard to top Hal Cooper's serial killer turn.

Our research for these files led us to a deep dive into the iconic institutions and landmarks that our suspects frequent. Imagine Riverdale without Pop's. It just simply wouldn't be the same. Where else do we expect the town residents to eat? We've certainly never seen a grocery store! Who are we kidding? You know that Alice Cooper subscribes to Blue Apron (#NotAnAd . . . yet).

You see, it is these places that make Riverdale the town it is. And just like the residents themselves, these institutions hide their sinister affairs behind seemingly innocent Americana fronts. We are here to bust down the doors that hold so many of these secrets. By exploring the town's most frequented haunts—along with its resident gang, its own historic murderer, and even a local illicit substance—we can have a deeper understanding of its citizens' psyches.

THE
SERPENTS

SERPENT MEMBERS

1. FP JONES (RETIRED)
2. JUGHEAD JONES
3. BETTY COOPER
4. THOMAS TOPAZ
5. TONI TOPAZ (EXILED)
6. SWEET PEA
7. FANGS FOGARTY
8. ~~PENNY PEABODY~~
9. BYRDIE
10. CHERYL BLOSSOM (EXILED)
11. ~~TALL BOY~~
12. SLASH
13. JOAQUIN DESANTOS (RIP)
14. MUSTANG (RIP)
15. HOT DOG

A s firm believers in not stereotyping a mass group of people, we cringe every time we hear a character refer to the Serpents as all being dangerous criminals who have set out to ruin Riverdale. Sure, they may ride loud motorcycles and lower your property value. But much like serpents themselves, if you do not bother them, they will not bother you.

We actually have zero idea how real serpents work and advise you to not trust us on this matter.

The Serpents are also technically the first group of people to settle in Riverdale. Long before General Pickens ever laid eyes on Sweetwater River, the land originally belonged to the Uktena tribe. Eventually the Uktenas evolved into the modern-day Southside Serpents, but this was not due to any sort of natural evolution. No, it was the result of genocide. The General Augustus Pickens whom the Northsiders hold in such high regard was a brutal murderer hired by Barnabas B. Blossom to slaughter the Uktena nation. Very few members of the original Uktena tribe still remain in Riverdale, but those who do are still haunted by the wailing of their ancestors.

It is this necessary drive for survival that has bonded the Serpents together and made them such a force to be reckoned with. Ironically enough, the gang's current leader is none other than a decidedly non-Uktenan member, Jughead Jones. And right next to him on the throne is his serpent queen, Betty Cooper.

Quite frankly, we have yet to fully recover from the serpent Dance that Betty had to complete for her initiation. We find it kinda funny, and we find it kinda sad. But that's why we love this show.

In our humble opinion, the best Serpent is Hot Dog, a gorgeous cuddly floof of a sheepdog who has been in the Serpent family for what feels like generations.

For the most part, the Serpents get a bum rap. However, when the head of the General Pickens statue disappeared on Pickens Day, it seemed pretty clear which group was to blame. Sheriff Keller was convinced that Jughead was the one who beheaded the statue of General Pickens, or at least knew the person who did it, and posted an eviction notice on FP's trailer. Sadly, FP and Jug were not the only ones facing eviction. Mayor McCoy was forcing the Serpents' entire trailer park to uproot to make way for the SoDale development because of this act of vandalism. Anatevka had nothing on the Southside.

Jughead took it upon himself to investigate who could be behind this beheading. Thankfully, the field of suspects narrows itself quite considerably when you consider that the person who committed the beheading would have to be strong and tall enough to handle a bronze head. With the assistance of an eyewitness, Betty and Jug discovered that it was in fact Tall Boy who beheaded General Pickens.

You see, Hiram Lodge had promised Tall Boy that the cops would come after the Southside if he stole the head. Knowing that this would inevitably lead to unrest, Tall Boy saw this as his opportunity to boot FP and Jughead out of the Serpents so that he could become their leader. We had our very own Southside *Macbeth* on our hands! The news of this attempted coup prompted the other Serpents to remove Tall Boy from the gang, but this would not be the last time that Tall Boy would strike.

On the night Hal Cooper confessed to being the Black Hood, yet another black hooded figure appeared at the Andrews house to attempt to kill Fred. The next morning, after receiving an anonymous tip, Sheriff Minetta went to question a suspect about the shooting. When he arrived on the scene, things immediately escalated into a firefight and the suspect was killed. The now-dead suspect ended up being none other than Tall Boy himself, who seemed to have gotten himself wrapped up in a pretty sticky situation after his removal from the Serpents. Sure enough, in Tall Boy's possession, law enforcement found guns that matched those used at the Andrewses' house and in the town hall shootings, along with a black hood.

With members like Tall Boy now out of the picture, many hope that the Serpents will go on to forge a new path. Hiram Lodge is going to be difficult to take down, and if the Northsiders and Southsiders want to survive his master plan, they are going to have to learn how to work together. Maybe then, once and for all, the entire town can see that the Serpents are not all that bad. Just maybe change the Serpent code before allowing more people to join. We don't know if we can handle watching the Serpent Dance one more time.

Years ago in Riverdale, there was a family of four that lived out by Fox Forest. They were just like every other family in Riverdale until one fateful evening when the Riverdale Reaper paid them a visit. This killer went into the family's home and shot them all dead. No one knows for sure what happened to this murderer after the shooting. While some believe that he was captured by a lynch mob, there are others who think that he hopped a train to California. Perhaps most frighteningly of all, some suggest that this monster never left Riverdale. Could the Riverdale Reaper and the Black Hood somehow be connected?

Sure enough, an old article about the Fox Forest murders in *The Riverdale Register* revealed that the family killed by the Riverdale Reaper was the Conways. More than that, it is discovered that the Conways' old house was where the Black Hood had sent Betty on a mission to find a black hood of her own that he left for her. With the help of Veronica and Archie, Betty and Jughead uncovered a lockbox containing old crime files inside the Conway house. Within this box was a crucial piece of evidence—an old family photo of the Conways revealing a third child who, until then, had been unaccounted for.

With further inspection it was discovered that the child's name was Joseph and he changed his last name when he was adopted by the Svenson family. Joseph Svenson. The school janitor. It seemed as though the one surviving member of the Conway family had been lurking around town this entire time. The question then, of course, was how did Joseph make it out of that house alive?

We later learn that Joseph Svenson apparently had heard the gunshots of the Riverdale Reaper inside his house and managed to sneak out a window. He waited outside just long enough to see the bloodied Riverdale Reaper leaving his house, and the next day, when the authorities asked a young Joseph who the killer was, he pointed out the man at a local motel. For a young Joseph Conway, this was his way of serving justice to the man who had killed his family; blood for blood. With the Riverdale Reaper's identity revealed, a group of men in town took the murderer away and buried him alive in Pickens Park.

If only the tale of the Riverdale Reaper could have ended this simply. It turns out that the man who should have been buried was the one doing the burying. For the real Riverdale Reaper was none other than Louis Cooper, Betty's grandfather. To clear his name, Louis convinced his son, Hal, to manipulate young Joseph Svenson into falsely accusing another man. Step aside, Annalise Keating, you're not the only one who can get away with murder.

POP'S CHOCK'LIT SHOPPE

While the *Riverdale* pilot was shot in an actual diner called Rocko's in Mission, British Columbia, ever since then the show has used a replica that was built in the studio parking lot. The studio is right off a major highway, and on more than one occasion there have been tractor trailers that have attempted to pull into Pop's, having mistaken it for a real-life diner. It looks *that* realistic!

Pop's Chock'lit Shoppe is the unofficial social center of Riverdale. Owned by Pop Tate, the diner has been in the Tate family for more than eighty years. A burger savant, Pop Tate needs only a few visits before your name, face, and exact order are ingrained in his memory.

While we are sure that you cannot go wrong with anything on the menu, *Archie* fans are well aware that you go to Pop's for the legendary burgers and milkshakes. It is truly a miracle, then, that everyone in Riverdale stays so fit! There must be some sort of magical fat-burning properties in that Sweetwater River water. *If that's the case, please bottle it and send it our way!*

To us, diners bring back memories of high school theater days gone by. After our high school plays would end, the only thing open in our suburban towns was always the town diner. Riding high from the adrenaline of a performance, you would always feel as though you could not possibly just go home and sleep. You HAD to go out and celebrate with your fellow castmates. Believe us, the post-show adrenaline still exists in theater people as they get older. They just trade chicken finger baskets at the diner for martinis at Glass House Tavern.

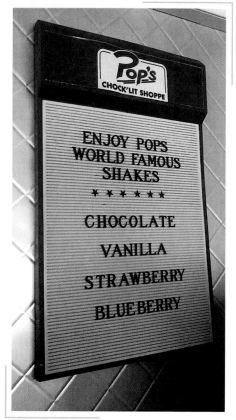

Actors who have scenes in Pop's can decide if they would like coffee or a milkshake! Production is also incredibly accommodating of dietary restrictions. Need your milkshake to be vegan? Don't worry! Pop's has got you covered!

Anyone want a gumball? PS: When is the last time you actually had a gumball?

That pinball machine actually works! Sometimes between takes the cast will try a round or two. While fun for those playing, the noise that emanates from the machine for minutes after it is touched is less fun for the director trying to get a shot without the sound of an old pinball machine.

We love a musical reference! Also, props to the Pop's restroom for being so progressive!

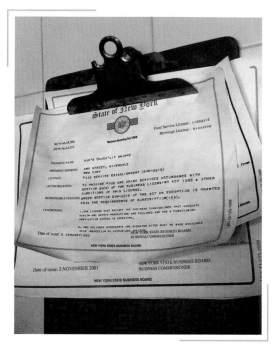

Fans have often speculated on the exact location of Riverdale. While this does not give us an exact location, take note that all the legal papers in Pop's are from the state of New York.

Every booth at Pop's holds an indelible memory of childhood days gone by. From post–football game celebrations to games of footsie underneath the table with your crush, the entire diner serves as a memory capsule.

Pop Tate is an instantly iconic character who has devoted his entire life to running his diner. When Hiram purchased the diner from the Tates, Pop's one request was that Hiram keep the purchase a secret as his mother was still alive and he knew how much it would pain her if she knew that the diner had left control of the family.

Listen, neither of us considers ourselves chefs by any stretch of the imagination. Still, we thought it would be fun to share a recipe of our own with you! As our listeners know, what we lack in food-preparation skills, we make up for with the cocktails that we offer all our guests on *Riverdish*! We've included a classic Pop's-style milkshake here, but for our twenty-one-plus readers, if you want to do this shake totally *Riverdish* style, add some bourbon!

Pop's Famous Maple Milkshake Recipe

PREP TIME: 5 minutes   READY IN: 3 minutes

1 scoop vanilla ice cream

1 scoop coffee ice cream

1 cup whole milk

1-2 teaspoons vanilla extract

1 teaspoon maple syrup

1 bar Toblerone chocolate, chopped

In a blender, add the scoops of vanilla and coffee ice cream, and then add the milk and vanilla extract. Blend until smooth. Add in the maple syrup and Toblerone bits, and blend again on a low speed. Once the texture is smooth, taste test! You can always add more maple syrup to your liking. Voilà!

At the end of season two, we witness Hiram hand over owner-
ship of Pop's to Veronica. And as if the diner couldn't get any more
iconic, Veronica decides to usher in a new era at Pop's by opening
a speakeasy in the basement called La Bonne Nuit. In true speakeasy fashion, one must enter through a pay phone booth located at
the back of the diner. Josie McCoy serves as the resident chanteuse
while Kevin Keller acts as the MC.

La Bonne Nuit is essentially Riverdale's
answer to Feinstein's/54 Below.

Entrance to La Bonne Nuit. Sadly, no one would give us the right number. Gave us major flashbacks to trying to get into PDT during our college years.

We LOVE a stage that REQUIRES you to make a grand entrance.

JINGLE JANGLE, OR JJ

KNOWN SIDE EFFECTS

Effects vary from person to person. Consumed via a paper straw, Jingle Jangle stays in your system for three days and can do irreparable damage. The drug creates a euphoric feeling in the user and keeps them up for days, in more ways than one.

Jingle Jangle gets its name from the title of the third album from the Archies, a fictional musical group from the original Archie Comics universe. If you haven't heard the song before, it is worth looking up! It's a total bop!

HISTORY OF THE DRUG

Jingle Jangle has plagued Riverdale for generations. Legend has it that the man who created and first sold the drug was named the Sugarman, and throughout the years, he has passed down his title and duties to the secret, special drug pushers who have taken over for him. Though mostly used and sold on the Southside, JJ has made its way north in a big way. Today, the drug is mostly sold through the Ghoulies, who get it into the hands of people around town. The last known Sugarman was Southside High teacher Robert Phillips, though he was exposed and subsequently arrested. It is unclear who is running the Jingle Jangle trade now, but if we had to place a bet, we would pin it on the crew behind Hiram's New Southside.

KNOWN PLACES OF ABUSE

- Lover's Lane with Midge and Moose

- The Five Seasons with Nick St. Clair

- The Last Resort hostel with Charles Smith and Chic

Riverdale High. This is an actual real-life public school located in the West Point Grey neighborhood on the west side of Vancouver, British Columbia, Canada. In addition to Riverdale High, the school has also served as Rosewood High in *Pretty Little Liars* and Finnegan High in *Mr. Young*.

It is easy to poke fun at the fact that the teenagers on *Riverdale* never actually attend classes, but this is, of course, a common trope among all teen shows. Classroom drama can take you only so far. Not every day in class can be filled with the dramatic tension of a group of prep school boys standing on top of their desks reciting "O Captain! My Captain!" à la *Dead Poets Society*. For most high schoolers the true drama takes place outside the classroom, so it makes sense that this is what we are shown. That being said, we have no idea when these kids actually have time to study or do homework. We thought it was hard juggling school-work with our after-school clubs and play rehearsals. We cannot imagine what it would be like adding a murder mystery on top of that.

Besides the occasional murders and riots, Riverdale High seems pretty similar to every other high school in the country. Though we would venture to say that most school cheerleading squads do not have special black funeral outfits. But then again, how many cheerleading squads are frequently asked to perform at funerals?

What Riverdale High has failed to teach their pupils in terms of book smarts, they have more than made up for in the street-smarts department. To survive Riverdale High, you have to keep your wits

This is actually the only classroom in Riverdale High! This room just gets re-outfitted with different decorations depending on what subject is being taught in each scene. Perhaps this is another reason why these teens never seem to be in class!

about you. If you have any sense, you know to never get on Cheryl Blossom's bad side. At least Principal Weatherbee seems easy enough to control. Strangely enough, he stood in full support of Archie's Red Circle group, even going so far as to defend the group to Sheriff Keller. We have a sneaking suspicion that there is more to Principal Weatherbee than we know. Too much is still unknown about him for him not to be hiding some skeletons in the closet.

As if there were not enough drama in the hallways of Riverdale High, the students now have to contend with a massive influx of transfer students pouring in from Southside High. We have to imagine that the school dances now look very similar to the "Dance at the Gym" sequence from *West Side Story*. Although this merge has had an understandably contentious beginning, we hope that by being forced to actually interact with each other, the youth of the north and south sides will be able to come together and unite against the evil powers of some of their older counterparts. The fact that Toni Topaz and Cheryl Blossom have already become such a united front shows promise for a more united Riverdale in the future. Like Whitney said, we believe that the children are our future. Now let's make sure that Riverdale High is actually teaching them well!

How awesome would it be if high school common rooms actually looked like this? Practically all the furniture on set has "Do Not Sit on the Furniture" signs . . . which the cast is known to often ignore. Oh well . . . they tried, right?

SWEETWATER
RIVER

Sweetwater River is not, in fact, a river at all! It is filmed at Alouette Lake, which is appropriately enough located in Maple Ridge, British Columbia, Canada.

I f New York City is the fifth character in *Sex and the City*, Sweet-water River is the hundredth character in Riverdale. The river serves as the border between Riverdale and Greendale and seemingly holds just as many secrets as the residents of the towns themselves. Along the river's edge, pine trees grow majestically toward heaven as if trying to break free of the ever-present fog that enshrouds the surrounding area.

For as picturesque as the river may seem, it is home to some of the town's most sinister events. It is here where Jason Blossom's dead body washed up on shore and where Archie Andrews heard a gunshot echo through the woods on the morning of July 4th. Of course, who could forget a suicidal Cheryl Blossom almost drowning underneath the river's thick layers of ice?

They say that time is like a river. You cannot touch the same water twice because the flow that has passed will never pass again. For generations, Sweetwater River has carried Riverdale's darkest secrets with it, but unlike the water passing through, these secrets will not be easily washed away.

S ince the beginning of time, developers have gravitated toward deteriorated neighborhoods with dollar signs in their eyes. Often acting as heroes, these investors swoop in with the promise of eliminating crime from the streets and bringing in new business. In the case of Riverdale, however, it seemed as though crime was the very thing that the so-called heroes were looking to perpetuate.

Hiram's office. As you can see, he's busy at
work on his plans for SoDale.

On the south side of Riverdale, the Lodge family was hard at work planning a series of new real estate developments. They called the project SoDale. SoDale promised to reinvent the Southside with more than fifty thousand square feet of commercial space, including luxury apartments, a shopping center, a movie theater complex, and even a golf course.

We know that technically we are not supposed to be rooting for SoDale, but we cannot help but dream about some of the amazing shopping opportunities that this development could provide for the town residents. All we want is to witness Alice Cooper walking through the aisles of Whole Foods.

Much is still unknown about the ultimate plans for SoDale. We know that Hiram is planning on turning Southside High into a for-profit prison and using some of SoDale to house the prison's employees. But does this mean that we are not getting any new shopping centers at all? We suppose there would be something strange about shopping for six-dollar asparagus water next to a prison, but still.

This is a real thing that was once sold at Whole Foods!

The people complaining about SoDale are the same as the old-school New Yorkers who long for the days when Times Square was filled with drugs and sex shops. Debatably the people in the Elmo costumes today are just as bad as the prostitutes who once stood in their place. But there is something nice about being able to catch a matinee of *Frozen* without having to worry about getting stabbed on the way out. Whether Hiram has similar aspirations for his development remains to be seen.

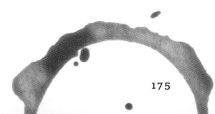

THE
WHYTE
WYRM

The Whyte Wyrm is a hole-in-the-wall bar in Riverdale's Southside. With its dilapidated walls and lived-in furniture, it has the look of a place that hasn't been cleaned in years, probably because it hasn't. The Wyrm has been the unofficial hangout of the Southside Serpents for years, and it is where all the Serpent Dances, initiations, and meetings have taken place.

The Whyte Wyrm would have been perfect for Lady Gaga's Bud Light Dive Bar Tour!

So much has gone down at the Wyrm. Who could forget that this is where Jason Blossom was murdered in the basement! If that's not a health code violation, we don't know what is.

Recently, the Wyrm was purchased by Hiram Lodge as part of his SoDale plan, and the basement was turned into a Jingle Jangle manufacturing plant operated by the Ghoulies. Long live the days of cheap booze and bad pole dancing.

The Whyte Wyrm is filmed at Gabby's Country Cabaret—a real-life karaoke joint in Langley, British Columbia, Canada. Can you imagine the Serpents doing karaoke? Just picture Sweet Pea belting out a rousing rendition of "Sweet Caroline." Or Cheryl and Toni duetting on "Total Eclipse of the Heart."

THORNHILL

E very town has one. The haunted house that inhabits the nightmares of every child. For the children of Riverdale, this house was Thornhill.

The Thornhill mansion was in the Blossom family for generations. Built by Claudius Blossom the first, the house sat on the far edge of town enshrouded by massive maple trees. If the Pembrooke is Riverdale's Buckingham Palace, Thornhill was its Taj Mahal. The home's backyard even included its own private graveyard, where countless members of the Blossom clan have been laid to rest.

After Jason's murder and Clifford's suicide, Cheryl Blossom took it upon herself to start anew. With a flick of her wrist, she lit Thornhill on fire, destroying her family home and sending her family's past up in flames. Now all that remains of the grand mansion is the somehow perfectly kept pool in the backyard. Because of course it is!

Since then, the remaining members of the Blossom clan have taken up residency at Thistlehouse. We suppose that the stakes of burning down your mansion are considerably lower when you have an equally nice mansion available to move in to.

The original Blossom home, Thornhill, was filmed at the Copper Stone Mansion. While incredibly dark and moody-looking in the show, the actual mansion is bright and stunning and has a private tennis court and swimming pool. In the season three premiere, we get the pool party at Thornhill we've been waiting for.

BEHIND THE SCENES

W hile investigating the endless crime in Riverdale, our research took us one step even further. Together, we have now studied these characters more intensely than anything else throughout our combined years of schooling and have uncovered a treasure trove of information about the history of the Archie Comics universe and the journey to the *Riverdale* series we all know and love. Let's dive in, shall we?

ARCHIE COMICS: A HISTORY

Since the 1940s, Archie, Betty, Veronica, and Jughead have been a staple of American pop culture. The characters have become as recognizable as Mickey Mouse, Bugs Bunny, and Superman. Say the name Archie Andrews, and we guarantee most will recall fond memories growing up reading the comic books or middle school years obsessing over Sabrina the Teenage Witch. The Betty vs. Veronica debate is still a hot topic among fans across the country. The legacy is timeless. But how did a gangly, freckled, red-haired teenager become an American icon?

It all started with three men. Back in 1939, Maurice Coyne, Louis Silberkleit, and John L. Goldwater founded a company with the primary goal of publishing superhero comics. The company was named

MLJ Magazines and published comics such as *The Shield*. Goldwater wanted to publish something more mainstream that featured non-superhero characters to appeal to the masses. In 1941, Archie Andrews and Jughead Jones were introduced to the world. The characters first appeared in the twenty-second issue of *Pep Comics* in 1941, written by Bob Montana and Vic Bloom.

An overnight success, MLJ published more and more *Archie* comics, eventually stopping the superhero characters completely. Within a few years, the company officially changed its name to Archie Comics, marking the start of an era.

Part of *Archie*'s appeal was due to Americans longing for an escape. In a time of war, Riverdale was a reminder of what Americans were fighting for: an idyllic town that represented the tranquility and hope of what America could be.

If they could only see the town now!

Archie Andrews was a normal teenager dealing with the ups and downs of high school and everyday life. People couldn't get enough.

Artist Dan DeCarlo entered the scene and modernized the look of the *Archie* characters in the late 1950s, defining the Archie and Gang we know and love today. After the death of Bob Montana, DeCarlo took over as chief artist and went on to create Josie and the Pussycats.

After the deaths of Louis Silberkleit and John Goldwater, Louis's son, Michael, and John's son Richard took over the company in the 1980s. Richard Goldwater died in 2007 and his half brother Jon took over as CEO of Archie Comics. It was then that big changes started to be made.

Jon Goldwater had a mission. He wanted to take the *Archie* comics and bring them into the new millennium. Instead of living in the nostalgia of the past, Goldwater wanted to set Riverdale in the present day by modernizing the characters again. Throughout his run, the risks he took paid off. Goldwater introduced zombies, homosexual characters, disabled characters, sci-fi, and witchcraft, among other things, into the world of Riverdale and forever changed the franchise.

DEVELOPING THE SHOW

For years, television and film executives attempted to bring the beloved *Archie* gang to the screen. Before *Riverdale*, there were countless failed pilots, pitches, and even a made-for-TV movie that featured Jughead rapping—pretty tragic.

Enter Roberto Aguirre-Sacasa.

A longtime *Archie* fan, Roberto grew up loving comics. In fact, he first came to the attention of Archie Comics when the company issued him a cease and desist letter over a play that he wrote entitled *Archie's Weird Fantasy*, in which the character of Archie moves to New York City and comes out of the closet. Understandably, the company took issue with how far the play had Archie stray from his traditional image. Eventually, the play took on the title *Golden Age*, and the character of Archie was changed to Buddy Baxter. It went on to receive glowing reviews from major publications like *The New York Times*, and in turn, Marvel Comics hired him to create a new Fantastic Four series.

Roberto continued to write and produce and went on to work on numerous projects, ranging from *Glee* to *Carrie, American Psycho:*

The Musical, *Spider-Man: Turn Off the Dark*, and *Supergirl*. We are personally most excited for his latest project as book writer for the upcoming *Magic Mike* musical. If the gratuitous shirtless scenes on *Riverdale* are any indication of what to expect, we can only imagine that audiences are in for a treat!

In 2013, Roberto created *Afterlife with Archie*, which depicted Archie and the gang in a whole new world—in the middle of a zombie apocalypse. This was notably the first *Archie* comic directed toward a more mature audience. The first eight issues sold out instantly and led to Roberto becoming the chief creative officer of Archie Comics, a position created for him to bring in new writers and develop fresh, exciting concepts for the Riverdale characters. It was when he was in this position that *Riverdale*, the TV show, was born. Roberto wrote the pilot in 2014 and brought on Greg Berlanti as a co-executive producer.

The show was pitched as the Riverdale everyone knows and loves but with much darker elements. Roberto combined elements of mystery, noir, and modern teen-soap drama to juxtapose our all-American gang against much more sinister story lines. He knew there needed to be a sharp edge to the show from the very beginning. It was also his idea to focus on the town itself rather than the characters. He wanted to explore how the characters would respond to the great evils that would come their way if the town were the root of the darkness. His idea was for a much more subversive, previously unseen take on the world of *Archie*.

Fox originally agreed to be the network for the show, but they ended up passing. After the show was shopped around networks for two years, Roberto's *Riverdale* finally landed at the CW. The green light was given, and the pilot quickly went into production.

PRODUCTION

The show films in Vancouver for eight to ten months throughout the year. A soundstage was constructed and hosts a number of sets used to film the world of *Riverdale*. Exteriors are shot in various locations throughout the city.

Stars! They're just like us! Most often, the cast takes a van to set together from downtown Vancouver. On their way, they always make sure to swing through the Starbucks drive-thru. While the staff is now accustomed to having them as customers, you can only imagine their initial surprise when the entire cast of *Riverdale* pulled up to the window.

CASTING

Casting the iconic *Archie* characters was no easy task. The initial character breakdown for the pilot already saw a departure from the traditional all-American characters. It depicted Betty as a pill-popping perfectionist, an emo heartthrob version of Jughead, a Latina Veronica Lodge desperate to reinvent herself, and an Archie Andrews skirting the fine line between his music and sports.

It took six months to cast the pilot. Cole Sprouse of Disney Channel fame was first approached to play Archie. But after reading the script, the star connected more to Jughead's outsider status. It was a role different from any he'd played before, so he jumped at the chance. For many of the young leads, *Riverdale* was their first big job. Camila Mendes, who plays Veronica Lodge, graduated from NYU's Tisch School mere weeks before she booked the job. Lili Reinhart got the part of Betty off a self-taped audition she recorded on a break from her job at Pier 1 Imports. She had previously worked in small roles but never a role of this size.

Finding Archie Andrews was the most challenging. After an extensive search, KJ Apa emerged as the only choice for the show's main character. He was cast three days before the network was due to test Archies for the studio. Apa is originally from New Zealand and not a natural redhead. *Riverdale* is his first US-based role.

RIVERDALE SHOW INFLUENCES

TWIN PEAKS

GOSSIP GIRL

JOHN HUGHES MOVIES

BLUE VELVET

RIVER'S EDGE

DAWSON'S CREEK

PLEASANTVILLE

ZODIAC

TALES FROM THE DARKSIDE

THE GODFATHER

PRETTY LITTLE LIARS

VERONICA MARS

STEPHEN KING NOVELS

STAND BY ME

TRUE DETECTIVE

THE END . . . FOR NOW

Well, there you have it, River Vixens! While we're probably not going to drop our day jobs for a life of solving crime, it was still fun to pretend for a little bit. This show throws so many twists and turns at its viewers that no matter how closely you keep tabs on all the characters and suspects, a new development is going to come out of left field anyway. But that is why we love this show.

The *Archie* comics started out with the goal of distracting their readers from everyday life. When the country was at war, the idyllic small-town lifestyle that the *Archie* characters maintained served as a reminder of what we were fighting for. Now, as the world has changed, so has *Archie*. The world of Riverdale is no longer the safe haven that it once was, but for its viewers, it still serves as a place of escape. As our world has turned even crazier, it is the insanity of *Riverdale* that now provides us with comfort.

Like generations before us, we are allowed a weekly check-in with our friends at Pop's. Though the crimes in town may be new, timeless elements like first loves, heartbreaks, and high school drama remain constant. There is a bit of Riverdale in every town.

And as for us? Well, as long as *Riverdale* keeps giving us new stories to follow, we will be here, ready to make sense of it all. And in the meantime, we'll be refining our songbooks for our eventual debut at La Bonne Nuit and trying to avoid any mass murderers.

("Lollipop" ringtone plays in the background.)

Well, we'd better be off, then. Stay safe, River Vixens!

ACKNOWLEDGMENTS

Ryan and Sam would like to express their endless gratitude to all who have made the *Riverdish* empire possible. When we first set out to create our podcast, *Riverdish,* it was a total labor of love. Little could we imagine the way that this show would ultimately affect our lives. To every guest who has joined us on mic and every listener who has put up with our craziness in their headphones, thank you.

Riverdish the book wouldn't be possible without our editor, Sean Newcott. There can be one hundred people in a room, and ninety-nine of them don't believe in you. All it takes is one person who does. And that, for us, was Sean. From meetings over milkshakes to endless emails, we could not have produced this book without her.

Along with Sean we must express our thanks to the entire team at Dey Street Books for all of their work: Jessica Lyons, Kendra Newton, Imani Gary, Andrea Monagle, Michelle Crowe, and Shelby Peak. Your support has meant the world.

We would also like to thank Casey Cott for putting up with us. From Marie's Crisis duets to boa-filled limo rides, we are shocked that you have yet to file a restraining order against us.

In no particular order, we'd also like to thank Matthew K. Begbie, Barbara Wallace, Cody Kearsley, Alvin Sanders, Julian Haig, the staff at Soho House, Meghan Markle and Prince Harry, Virginia Ashe, Grace Link, Courtney Alexander for letting us always record the pod LOUDLY in the apartment, the clams, Brian Patrick Murphy, Michael Littig, the cast of *The Real Housewives of New York City*, *SpongeBob: The Musical*, gay Twitter, Cathay Pacific, the Flying Pig restaurant chain in Vancouver (except for the one waitress who called Sam out on finishing an entire salad), Dean Patrick Murphy, the Hamptons Jitney, Greg Nobile, Oliver Roth, David Manella, Nick Rizzo, Eric Maxwell, Kira Frank, Sydney Epstein, Blanche Boisvert-Light, Monet Sabel, Louis Peitzman, Natalie Walker, Rachel Gold, Cole Delbyck, Jackson McHenry, Emily Tannenbaum, Kyle Fox, Kyle Selig, Molly Fitzpatrick, Brian Moylan, Ryan O'Connor, Mark Mauriello, Danny Pellegrino, Ryan McPhee, John Trowbridge, Sophie Santos, Jake Boyd, Josh Groban, Michael Gioia, Sarah Hinrichsen, Jenny Baker, Andrew Keenan-Bolger, Elana Siegel, Kaitlyn Herman, Alex Temple Ward, the Tony Awards, Naomi at Southern Hospitality, the creators of *Search Party*, the Hard Rock Café, Shanice Williams, Todd, the Carlyle, the *Today* show, Feinstein's/54 Below, Goop, Seamless, Cabernet Sauvignon, *Bright Star*, pools, the salesgirls of "Courtney, Take Your Break," Dan Shinaberry, the margaritas in Hell's Kitchen, and Nikki Blonsky.

Ryan would like to thank his parents, John and Pat, along with his sisters, Tess, Ellie, and Hanna, for all of their support. Lastly, he would like to thank [insert name of rich future husband here]. Love ya, babe.

Sam would like to thank her parents, Susan and David, two rock-star humans who introduced her to the wonders of books at a very young age with the acclaimed novel *Samantha the Snob*. She'd also like to thank her lovely siblings, Emma and Moose. Emma is the coolest, most awesome person she knows, and Moose is the most handsome dog in all the land. Last but not least, the biggest thank-you to her partner in crime, Evan, for putting up with her as she rises to author superstardom. She loves you and our future woof, Gary, a lot. Even though you didn't look at her book contract.

IMAGE CREDITS

Retro line art illustrations: *RetroClipArt /Shutterstock, Inc.*

Snake illustration: *MicroOne /Shutterstock, Inc.*

Burger and milkshake illustrations: *SureWinners /Shutterstock, Inc.*

Camera illustration: *handini_atmodiwiryo /Shutterstock, Inc.*

File folder: *David Smart /Shutterstock, Inc.*

Post-it notes: *Lina Truman /Shutterstock, Inc.*

Gray lined paper: *windu /Shutterstock, Inc.*

Yellow lined paper: *Dewitt /Shutterstock, Inc.*

White notepaper: *Lu Wenjuan /Shutterstock, Inc.*

Blue index card: *optimarc /Shutterstock, Inc.*

Smoky background: *Alexander Marushin /Shutterstock, Inc.*

Coffee rings: *Vladimir Borozenets /Shutterstock, Inc.*

Milkshake photo: *bestv /Shutterstock, Inc.*

RYAN BLOOMQUIST is a performer and writer based out of New York City. If you have seen a regional production of *Les Misérables* within the past ten years, you have probably watched him die on a barricade. He is a graduate of NYU Tisch's New Studio on Broadway and can often be found spending far too much time on Twitter (@ryanbloomquist) and falling down deep YouTube rabbit holes of amateur productions of *Legally Blonde: The Musical*.

SAMANTHA GOLD is a New York City–based talent manager and producer, formerly of E! News and Creative Artists Agency. She is a graduate of Emerson College. Her work ranges from film/TV production to live events, talent wrangling, documentary editing, and podcasting. She did not direct the musical *Fun Home*.

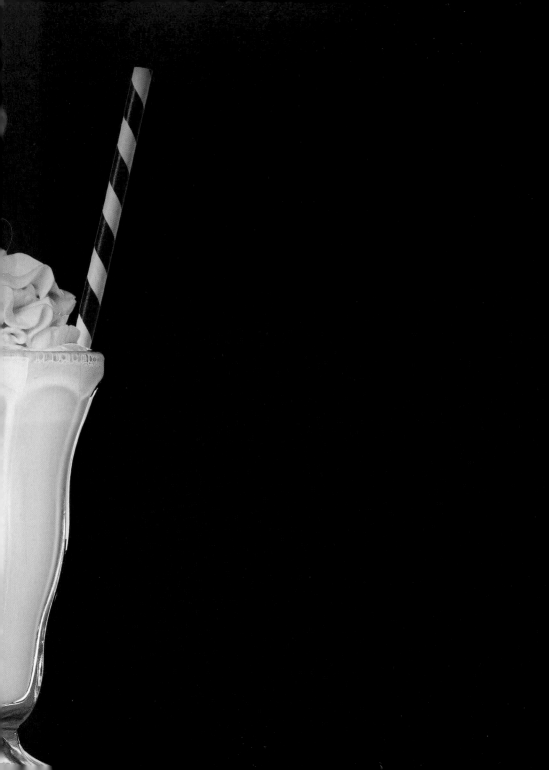